MARK ROBBINS

Princeton Architectural Press

Angles of Incidence

Princeton Architectural Press, Inc.
37 East 7th Street
New York, New York 10003
212.995.9620

To my parents

Editing and layout: Clare Jacobson
Cover design: Alexa Mulvihill
Special thanks to Joseph Cho, Antje Fritsch,
Stefanie Lew, Laura Mircik, Erika Updike,
and Ann C. Urban—Kevin Lippert

Library of Congress Cataloging-in-Publication Data
Robbins, Mark, 1956–
        Angles of Incidence / Mark Robbins.
            p.   cm.
        Includes bibliographical references.
        ISBN 1-878271-67-9
        1. Robbins, Mark, 1956–   —Themes, motives.
    2. Architecture, Modern—20th century—United
    States. I. Title.
    NA737.R55A4 1992   92-29640
    720'.92—dc20   CIP

Partial support for the production of this book was
provided by The Graham Foundation, Chicago
Illinois and the Ohio State University Columbia
Quincentenary Committee, Columbus, Ohio.

Contents

Preface
Mark Robbins

Back from town. Estates above the water, overlooking the bluffs, found on unfamiliar roads in winter. At the lake's edge the complex mix of thoughts remembered from the shore—fresh cold air, ice on rocks, the white lines of a water break parallel to the sand. In the parking lot, a woman reads a newspaper alone in her car with the sun light warming her face. She scans the flat blue-green expanse, out through the tinted windshield. Waiting. Another woman in a car sleeps. Couples walk on the sand from one set of locked park structures to another. I notice the single people. The man in the windbreaker, tied over a thick middle, glasses, thin soled shoes. A walk up the shore to a vacant building? A men's room? A guy—blonde, distracted—sits in his car, the window rolled down half way. I am interested in both. A series of narratives, base and romantic. I question the authenticity of the reverie, like the imitation fascination with the birds in the Ramble at Central Park. Both innocent to the world and playing it.

On the Safe Side, 1974
Super 8mm film

Colgate, 1976
Super 8mm film

I think again about fiction after reading some short, fairly personal accounts of life in the Midwest by contemporary authors who have lived there. (Most persist in a guarded view of the region, frozen in the depression era voice of the Writers' Project. The images are Paul Strand and Dorothea Lange, rust and peeling wood siding.) I think about my wanting to tell stories, both fiction and enhanced truth. Ambiguous stories, abstractions that are read in many ways. Sergei Eisenstein talks about the engagement of an audience in film through an active intercutting of the narrative, and I think about the construction of the films that I made while still in school. After screenings shown to small audiences, I interpreted the silence of the viewers as a sign of their having been moved, a break before resuming real time. This is what I wanted to achieve through these

non-narrative, rhythmic films. Influenced by the editing strategies of Peter Kubelka and the form and content of Stan Brakhage and Kenneth Anger they were full of images that I found of "universal" power. A naked figure of a keening woman, a fellow student taking off a white shirt, heavyset families in a public park in northern Appalachia. These were intercut with more neutral background elements to develop a rhythm of hot and cool images; figure and ground.

Performance: Natchez, MS, 1987; Wigstock, NY, 1990

So I frame these experiences in architecture like film or performance—a Wagnerian scope to the work, a melodrama, a documentary that begs truth. In those early films Life and Death and the World were condensed into fifteen minutes, in 250 edits. The compression, and allure, of a TV commercial with other "lite" motifs. In a recent installation, the experience was accompanied by light, music, narration, opening and closing views. Pushing the interactive component, the spectator is engaged in the creation of the scene.

What I show here in this small book is the work of the past twelve years, from early films to drawings, objects, and installation projects. The chronology and editing of the work is a convenience that, in its ordering and omissions, provides the appearance of a single consistent line, a progression that was in fact less clear. The publication is a way to frame that work to date.

The earliest objects in the book are small containers, boxes. They reveal my fascination with condensed and complete worlds, like those depicted in the dioramas I saw each Saturday afternoon at the Museum of Natural History. Those brightly lit windows are filled with the skins of animals stretched over plaster armatures, the space receding back into a jungle or tundra or a climax forest in North America; the foreground is cleverly separated from the perspectival painting (even in the odd ethnographic tableau of a Dutch governor meeting dark skinned men to purchase Manhattan, the fort in the background).

Bongo
Museum of Natural History

Shop window, New York

Around the time of these visits I saw a long, hinged cacao pod at a flea market. The interior showed an apartment building in section, the inhabitants engaged in activities oblivious to the events in the other spaces—my own view. It recalls, now, sectional movie sets (like that for *The Diary of Anne Frank*), built as half houses to reveal the interior, maintaining the appearance of enclosed space, without ceiling or wall to accommodate the mobile camera. This accommodation of the viewer within the construction of the film mirrors the view from across the space of the street or air shaft in the city. Alfred Hitchcock exploits this in *Rear Window*. The voyeur of the binoculars is in fact the camera, which stands in for the audience's eye. Perhaps Hitchcock refers to an earlier pictorial tradition that situates the eye of the viewer in a painting of the Dutch School.[1] The placement of a mirror or the outward glance of the subject breaks the frame, the barrier between the self-contained space and the milieu of the painted scene. The viewer is implicated, in the spatial extension of the gaze, beyond the confines of the picture plane.

My later installation projects expand the representation of space to habitable proportions. I have attempted to retain a cultural density in this built work. Compared to film and painted representation, architecture may seem an inflexible medium of expression. But buildings and spaces are encoded with meaning and are not neutral. They perpetuate and participate in a given order, reinforce authority, encourage affiliation, etc. This occurs within vernacular, commercial, and high architecture.

St. Jerome in his study

Laundromat, 10th Avenue

Most telling, perhaps, is commercial architecture, which renders certain stylistic characterizations repeatedly, providing shorthand for a given landscape and era. This architecture, like media and political offerings, trades on easy-to-read symbols. A stock set of elements is reused, breeding a weaker strain of quotations applied in an increasingly remote mix of veneers, at multiple scales regardless of building type, context, or region (Mansard meets Tudor in stucco, on a four-family colonial town home, without irony). This thin eclecticism offers a calming homogeneity, asserts historical continuity, and raises no questions. It recalls the Bob Evans tag line: "the way it was is the way it is"—a static present resting on a simplification of the past.

Family dining

Coexistent with these theme settings is the preponderance of the ordinary, un-styled spaces of back offices and cut-rate shopping centers. Rather than the romanticized decay of roadside ruins, it is blue-light specials and shrink-wrap. The day is spent on bridges and highway cloverleaves, flooded with signage set against the mirrored walls of count-

Wellsberg, West Virginia

Roadside—Cambridge, Ohio

less interchange industrial parks. This entire collection of built form provides a rich text reflecting past and current aspirations, where mythology meets life on the ground. Both categories of architecture—the self-conscious and the functional—provide artifacts for representation.

This reading of American architecture—one that looks at elements that are readily consumed by the American public, often without choice, for their

Advertising

places of residence and entertainment—goes beyond false consciousness and Formica. It embraces textures, materials, and interior and urban spatial conditions that can be derived from the landscape at hand. There is a sense in this work of an American distillation: motel rooms, bright cars, plastic trim, thin modern walls laminated with information, and the flashing of popular media alongside sleek, soundless technology. These have iconic representational value and are a basis for abstraction.

My work stresses transformation of an initial subject as a way to synthesize historical forms with current production. Elements are excised from traditional contexts and bring traces of meaning into a new assemblage. Through a juxtaposition of frame with discordant space and image a critical position may be generated. I have attempted to construct work that can break the dullness of habit in the perception of the built world, take buildings from the distracted periphery of perception, and use the impact of setting and spatial typologies to allow construction to participate in lived experience in a richer way. Architectural form has the inherent power, to signify (more readily recognized in the other arts) and to communicate matters of substance about the culture in which it is produced.

Lake Forest, Illinois, 1992

1. This point follows from a thesis asserted by W. Jude LeBlanc which ties the work of Hitchcock to that of Vermeer.

Acknowledgments

The projects in this volume have not been produced alone. Assistance in getting the work built has extended from hammering nails to incisive criticism. This has occurred with regularity since my earliest work in New York, and continues today in Columbus, Ohio.

I would like to thank some of the many people who have been so gracious with their time and interest and to my friends who have always shown up over the years. First among them are my collaborator Benjamin Gianni, for his sustaining support and enlightenment, and Brian McGrath for his early encouragement and continuing critical dialogue about the value of the city and seeing America first.

Given the current threat to local and national sponsorship of the arts I would also like to thank the foundations and individuals who have enabled diverse work to develop in many fields. In my own work this has included The New York State Council on the Arts, which has provided repeated support over the past ten years; special thanks to Deborah Norden for her long-term consideration of this work. The New York Foundation for the Arts and The Ohio Arts Council, as well as Penny Dannenberg and Pat Henahan of their respective staffs, have been most supportive. The Design Arts Program of the National Endowment of the Arts provided initial support for the "Framing American Cities" project, with great assistance from Tim Fitch.

The Architectural League was an early forum for this work and I thank Rosalie Genevro, its executive director, for her energy and clear insights. In addition I would like to acknowledge the unique settings that allowed me time to create. The MacDowell Colony and the Ragdale Foundation both provided the necessary space to write, sketch, and think.

I first taught at Ohio State University in 1986 and became a full-time faculty member in 1990. The affiliation has been fruitful and both the School of Architecture and the Department have been generous in support of my research. I would like to thank Robert Livesey for innumerable letters and Jose Oubrerie for support and time to accomplish these projects. Several of my colleagues at Ohio State and The Parsons School of Design have read and reviewed some of this material. Jeff Kipnis merits particular thanks. Cicily Horan, Joyce Starr, and Vi Schaaf deserve note for their administrative attention and patience. Students of both schools have provided questions and clarification for the material at hand. Those who have been so committed in their work on many of the projects in the book include Tom

Easterson, Diane D. Porthouse, Phillip L. Rudy, Lewis D. Huffman, Tom Pitzen, Steve Turk, Maria Ramirez, Mark Noltimier, Kevin Kemner, Dan Grandy, Bill Markland, and Ben Felix.

Other persons have had an impact on the formation of the work. Susana Torre encouraged me to pursue the content of the early architectural constructions. Her support and her interpretations have been invaluable. Hours spent with Dennis Dollens over coffee and texts sparked ideas about architecture and the importance of a political stance. Mickey Friedman's interest gave me the opportunity in *Design Quarterly* to crystallize many of the ideas translated into the final form of "Framing American Cities." This last project has been in development since 1986 and early written support came from Emilio Ambasz, James Stewart Polshek, and Susana Torre.

I am appreciative of the Institute of Contemporary Art and its former director Tom Finkelpearl for bringing the first leg of this installation to the Clocktower Gallery in New York. The Wexner Center for the Arts has made the production of the three cities in the final installation possible. Sarah Rogers-Lafferty, Senior Curator, has been a supporter of this work and the exhibition from an early stage in its evolution. Annetta Massie and the construction crews and staff at the center have been assets throughout this long process.

Finally I would like to thank those most specifically involved with the production of this volume. Friends and essayists Patti Phillips, who provided continuity and support in my tenure at Parsons School of Design, and Pat Morton, who has suggested alternate readings of my work, as well as Benjamin Gianni have my deep gratitude for their sharp and thoughtful essays. Special thanks to Diane D. Porthouse for her help in assembling this book, Anne Bremner of the Wexner Center for a fresh editorial eye, and Alan Jazak for his graphic sense. At Princeton Architectural Press, thanks are due to Kevin Lippert for his receptiveness to this material and to Clare Jacobson for her careful editing and design of this book and for shepherding this project through to completion.

Prospect For Architecture

Patricia C. Phillips

For over a decade, Mark Robbins has pursued a searching, skeptical architectural practice. His curiosities and convictions embrace occupancy (a subject that preoccupies most architects) and observation—in both its accepted and unsanctioned forms. Architectural programs typically center on use, activities, function, and expectations. Robbins' programmatic preoccupations involve behaviors and perceptions that architecture frequently conceals—and only inadvertently exposes.

For all of the reputed structural integrity and material honesty of modernism, the mimetic glass and steel skylines and facades of corporate-fed American cities offer only an illusion of transparency and privileged vision. Glass, in fact, proves to be a particularly uncooperative messenger of open exchange; it frustrates unobstructed, unedited views. In contrast, Robbins' use of common materials and construction practices exposes the occupant and observation; it enables the observation of occupancy.

Robbins orchestrates a discursive architectural syntax shaped by modern theory and vernacular builders. He does not reject modernism but challenges its purification of program. He appropriates—and then revises—its vocabulary of order so that sight is not slighted or silenced. In a restless range of projects dramatically varied in scale and situation, Robbins presents an architecture that discloses and makes manifest the worlds of structures and systems—and of our experiences of them—that have been quietly tucked away and conveniently hidden from sight. Through quietly subversive strategies, he exposes the repressive program and the deliberate limitations of most accepted architectural tautologies. Inspired by the problems of architecture and cautious of its manipulatable instrumentality, Robbins is a faithful skeptic. He values the communicative potential of architecture at the same time that he finds many of its prevailing notions spurious.

There are two unrelated and incongruous structures that offer access to Robbins' work. Whether they, in fact, are acknowledged influences is less important than their demonstration of the ways that architecture diagrams perceptual experiences, a cosmological view of the world, and a personal vision.

The first structure comes out of the nineteenth- and early twentieth-century New York environs. As industrial momentum began to portend an increasingly constricted urban situation, bucolic viewing pavilions were constructed along the Hudson River and in other spectacular natural settings. These little buildings offered places of respite and reminders of nature's incalculable forces; they served as beautiful antitheses to the sublime magnificence of the congested city.

Situated on dramatic promontories, these modest architectural interventions were small outdoor rooms with solid backs and roofs overhead. Normally, the facade was an open frame bordered by supporting columns and a low balustrade. Visitors could sit or stand to gaze at a designated landscape outlined by the formal architectural elements of the carefully composed building.

This viewing prototype was the building as frame. Except for the promise of short-lived, quiet retreat, it supported no other purpose than the apotheosis of the natural view beyond the rectangular edges of the particular building—and the alarming encroachments of the modern city. The architecture established the terms and formed the acceptable boundaries by which the visitor would see and consider a (diminishing) landscape. In a disquieting inversion, the viewer occupied an intimate proscenium in order to see the selected spectacle beyond the building's silhouette. Architecture as outlook was a lens on a romanticized, pastoral scene.

The architecture of observation also can be aggressively introspective and intensely urban. In Amsterdam the "red light district" embraces the idea of the gaze and gives it spatial and economic authority. In conspicuous contrast to the bucolic, escapist viewing pavilions situated on the Hudson's Palisades, Amsterdam's active urban neighborhood frames vision, excites desire, and feigns escape. The spaces of prostitution are simply another version of vision—another concept of view as expectation.

Red light district, Amsterdam

Red light district, Amsterdam

Women engaged in selling sexual services sit in small, street-front rooms, each programmatically and formally faithful to the established typology. Each observation "pavilion" has a glass door adjacent to a large, "picture" window. Within the frame of the window, the women sit, often pressed close to the glass, on a chair or stool. Like a carefully rendered composition, figure and ground, foreground and background are skillfully negotiated. Each woman's figure—her face, body, hair, skin, and clothing—are the seductive accouterments of the foreground. In the background a neatly made bed serves as a more subliminal advertisement. The message is "what you see is what you get."

When a consumer/customer decides on a particular transaction, he or she enters the room. Shades are quickly drawn on the door and window. They remain this way until the brief encounter is completed and the "guest" leaves. Then the shades are raised or parted, the woman resumes her position on the chair to wait for the next client. In the old medieval city of dense, meandering streets, there are repeated rows of these little chambers. In streets, some fewer than six feet wide, the view provided is not indirect; it is intense and introverted. This is life documented with a macro lens; the wide-angle is of a different setting—and century.

These serene and steamy viewing pavilions are exceptional examples of a dioramic architecture—of the carefully constructed picture, the invented scene. Whether the subject is nature or sex, archi-

tecture isolates and intensifies a singular, focused prospect. The view is the commodity and architecture is the instrument.

In contrast to these sites of surveillance, the architectural environments that Robbins establishes for the viewer/participant are never so contained, deterministic, or inevitable. There is always a spatial and material dimension manifest, but there is a much larger, unbounded, and unregulated domain of insinuation by encounter. One may leave the pavilion or enter the cubicle and draw the shades; the actual evidence of the view is gone. But the evocation, the startling potency of imagination and memory breach the segregation of walls—the absence in architecture. Robbins constructs his practice in this immaterial but resonant domain of recollection and sensation.

In much the same way that the traditional viewing pavilion or the Dutch "red light district" inscribes the behavior of the individual within larger social and political systems, Robbins' work negotiates the human body and the body politic, the single citizen and the surrounding community. The scale shifts; the quiet interrogation of new observations always places perception and experience somewhere between private and public, intuition, and reason.

Whether constructing small night tables that conflate the issues of domestic politics and personal memories into a single object, or pursuing an urban project that embraces the topographic conditions and planning histories of three American cities, Robbins' work provides a direct access to often difficult, disquieting issues of visual engagement and dispossession. His work is an implication that our own views and vision are passionately nurtured yet subject to unrelenting doubt.

Although the work has intellectual dimensions that transcend circumstantial evidence and specific region, American social and spatial environments are the genesis of many projects. Some of the influences are directly lifted from literature or context. For example, Robbins' project "Winesburg, Ohio" (1989, done in collaboration with architect Benjamin Gianni) is two related speculations on discrete voyeurism, social roles, and frustrated desire. The project is a meditation on a chapter called "The Strength of God" in Sherwood Anderson's classic novel of small town American life. In quiet vigil, a minister spies through a hole he has made in the leaded glass window of his parish's belfry. On several occasions, he gazes at the bare neck and shoulders of the town's young school teacher as she lies on her bed. In a final, anguished moment of

voyeurism, the minister spies the naked woman as she prays in despair. Through the minister's eyes, her young body suddenly appears as the figure of Christ; lust and salvation become indivisible. This stark, eloquent moment of secret longing is explored in wooden structures that imply the architectural apparatus of forbidden vision—the belfry, the pulpit, the window, and the bed—but applies them in an amended, abstract, and accepting way.

In 1991, Robbins and Gianni built a room-sized installation entitled "Signs and Wonders" in the Hewlett Gallery at Carnegie Mellon University in Pittsburgh. Here, the generative idea involved two former residents of the western Pennsylvania city— the faith healer and evangelist Kathryn Kuhlman, and the artist and Pop guru Andy Warhol. Kuhlman's and Warhol's theatrical manipulations of their respective media informed the architects' interactive environment. Viewers scaled the piece, carried props, and became players in their own theatrical event. To see is to witness; to know is to question what is actually seen. "Winesburg" explores covert, clandestine desire; "Signs and Wonders" illuminates explicit, consuming possession. All viewers become involved, if not impartial, observers of vision as a process of dedicated deliberation.

In his only outdoor project, "Utopian Prospect," (1988), Robbins pursued the idea of the viewing pavilion yet applied an unusual syntax of architectural conventions. The view is preeminent, but it was purposefully complicated and destabilized. Here architecture produces multiple visions rather than the inviolable template of a single view. The project is sited in Woodstock, New York on the grounds of the Byrdcliffe Art Colony. Rather than creating an architectural shelter with a fixed frame, Robbins made a viewing pavilion that is a wall punctured and amended. The use of the wall as a viewing instrument is the architect's first ironic involution. The embedded siting—an incestuous relation to the landscape—is another. Rather than an element sitting astride the landscape, the wall is actually a deep sectional slice in the sloping site.

Robbins begins with a wall and undermines its divisive opacity. Two apertures are punched out of the thick, free-standing block structure. The smaller, lower window is covered by a grate. On one side of the wall it sits two feet off the ground. From the other side, a narrow stairway has been excavated deep into the site. At the base, a person can stand and look comfortably through the mesh-clad opening—scanning just above ground level.

Nineteenth-century prison auditorium, France

Above this, at chest-height and slightly off-center, a larger window with steel mullions and an operable shutter frames more conventional views of the environment. On the side of the wall opposite the sunken stairs is a cantilevered wood slab. This is Robbins' ironic homage to the bench of the classic viewing pavilion—and yet another site from which to apprehend the landscape. Unlike the enclosed, protected point of view established in the earlier pavilions, the view from this bench is open and exposed, but quietly controlled. The bench's exterior placement fixes the position of the viewer but enhances the possible angles of vision. Not far from the wall a small brick tower supports a swinging vane. On one arm is an open frame for isolating certain passages and moments of vision. On the other a mirror alternately reflects the wall, the viewer, other participants, and the site. Robbins' "Utopian Prospect" constructs the quixotic time of vision rather than an unyielding space of the view. The wall is an implication of—rather than an obstruction to—the experience of active seeing. Unlike the controlled space of the traditional viewing pavilion, the open space of Robbins' project is about watching others see so that landscape is experienced fully through one's own eyes and the imaginative references of others' encounters.

Robbins' most recent and most temporally and spatially dynamic project, "Framing American Cities" (1986–) is a social and morphological investigation of three American cities—New York, San Francisco, and Columbus, Ohio. This trilogy of urban sites illuminates the relation of geography to urban patterns, western migration to the habits of settlement, and physical form to regional and social contingencies. But the underlying prospect of the project is evoked by its title. "Framing" concerns the ways that people negotiate urban scenes and private vision, city images and direct experience.

The inaugural installation of this multiple, accretive proposition occurred in New York at The Clocktower, Institute for Contemporary Art. The installation consisted of dyadic parts. The central spaces of the gallery were occupied by large, participatory structures. One included five tall, manipulatable towers set on a raised grated platform. The various components and materials—taut sheaths, louvered cavities, television monitors, a great sinewy knot of wires and cables—suggested the vast systemic and often invisible realities of the modern city. This place was a visceral, active counterpoint to the immateriality of contemporary life. Its brazen physicality created an intellectualized experience of urbanism.

Nearby, a maze of chambers with bare bulbs and other generic, institutional amenities released indismissive evidence of the psychological consequences of the modern bureaucracy. One's mind became numbed as one's body moved through the menacing monotony. Here, the corporeal components launched a direct assault. The only salvation from the dulling effects were subtle tricks and operable devices that permitted participants to affect the space—to move windows, to activate lights.

Operating parenthetically, Robbins installed a dyad of viewing arenas to observe these two sites. One was a steep, narrow set of bleachers. Viewers could sit and gaze at the local spectacle. Raised above the gallery floor, they were offered a more privileged view of the architectural proceedings. Even when unoccupied, the bleachers were an evocation of many viewers—of the scanning encounter of the panorama. On the other side of the gallery, an alternate viewing experience framed a brilliant and ironic moment of reverie. A narrow stairway, similar to the depressed stairs of "Utopian Prospect," scaled the gallery wall. At the top, a single viewer/participant could look through a slot (cut through the building's outer wall) to the bedazzling city beyond—seen reflected in a small hand mirror. This very singular, solitary experience of sight negotiated—framed—the intimacy inherent in all public space.

For many, architecture is used to maintain and separate private and public, domestic and political territories. Our built structures substantiate a world of privilege, exclusion, and control. Robbins' discursive productions offer a finely-honed lens and uncompromised focus to study the social and sexual regions of the built environment. Without casting the direction of the sight lines, the projects offer participants opportunities to see the affects of social and spatial conventions.

In "American Fictions" (1989), done in collaboration with Gianni and installed at the John Nichols Gallery in New York, the comforting sounds, the reassuring feel of the screened porch door, and the familiar proportions of the door frame lead to a claustrophobic space where vision is a conflicted, complicated experience. Like in the sex streets of Amsterdam, there was a long line of similar doorways and an atmosphere of edgy anticipation. In "American Fictions" the viewer stepped through a door to occupy a small cubicle that faced a bronzed canvas sheath. Like the drapes on a body prior to surgery, small openings were made strategically at the level of the eye and the genitals. The uneasy occupant gazed at small architectural objects while stealing glimpses of the unchoreographed motion of other bodies. Like the preacher in Anderson's searching narrative, the participant observes without being seen. The combative emotions of delight and torment in unsanctioned observation provide the psychological flavor of this uneasy environment.

Ways of seeing are inflected by architecture. And architecture is formed by prevailing political, class, and sexual assumptions. The distortions of sight, perpetuated to confirm a dominant view, are inscribed on—and by—the built environment. Robbins' work offers other perspectives of analysis, interpretation, and implication. Inevitably, "what you see is what you get." Robbins eloquent, oppositional work is an optimistic prospect for the potential of vision—for seeing what it is we really desire and require from architecture.

Guilt by Association: Notes by a Collaborator

Benjamin Gianni

Joseph Cornell, *Untitled "MedeciBoy,"* 1953

At first glance the small constructions of Mark Robbins bear the influence of the work of Joseph Cornell. Like Cornell's boxes, these pieces are condensed worlds composed of two-dimensional images, cutouts, frames, and three-dimensional objects. Like the lens of a human eye, the pieces focus projections of the world into concentrated, brain-like volumes. The constricted space of each of these volumes forces elements into proximity, and this proximity spawns associations. Robbins' pieces are reflective versions of the world. In them associations play back and forth as in a daydream or in free association. As if activated by a play of mirrors or a short circuiting of neural impulses, meanings loop and proliferate within the pieces. The semantic nuances that emerge are a function of spatial and syntactical relationships.

In a number of Robbins' pieces the components are arranged within a structured architectural framework, such as the triptych (see *Triptych* [pp. 22–23] and *The White Box* [pp. 28–29]). The fixity of the framework opposes the associative structure of the components. While the frame suggests hierarchy, the components within the frame resist such ordering. As such the components become place holders—supernumeraries in a production in which the principal actors are assumed to be missing. Being far from neutral, however, each place holder brings with it a set of associations. The production expands into a number of simultaneous productions, each sponsored by and undermining the architectural frame.

The interpreting mind does not easily accept the presence of such components as accidental or inadvertent. Because the frame marks the construction as a "work of art," the observer projects intention into each of its relationships. Whether these relationships are intentional or inadvertent (or intentionally inadvertent), their framing as "art" indicates that they are the outcome of conscious choices on the part of the author/artist. The piece, then, is recognized as an event to be deciphered. The viewer works to construct a meaningful relationship between the characteristics of a given element and the place it holds. The mind attempts to reconcile slippages and apparent inconsistencies between the structure of the frame and the elements that appear within it.

Again recalling those of Cornell, Robbins' constructions address the idea of the frame on two levels: manipulating conventions associated with framing an object as "art," and manipulating the frame as a device within the artwork. The outer frame designates the piece as art, and in so doing prompts interpretation; the frames within the piece direct interpretation toward the outer frame and establish framing as the theme of the piece. The piece, then, is both framed and about framing. On the broadest level, it is about conventions of interpretation, which are signaled through conventions of representation such as adjacency, homology, and framing.

It would be appropriate to characterize these pieces as postmodern given their tendency to frame meaning as a predominantly structural event. While all "significant" works of art operate on a structural as well as a semantic level, and while art can never be reduced to a message (just as a story is never independent of its telling), the characterization of these pieces as postmodern indicates the degree to which the structural is emphasized over the semantic, or the degree to which the semantic dimension (the *meaning*) is experienced as a by-product of structural relationships between components. In such works *meaning* is experienced as the *production of meaning*, and is recognized as a function of the mechanisms that produce it. The "what" (semantic dimension or reference) is overtaken by the "how" (structural or syntactical), as the mechanisms of meaning are forced into the viewer's consciousness. The piece is not only about the production of meaning, but its subject is recognizable as such.

Guilt by Association

This interest in the semantic impact of compositional structure can be compared to the work of Marcel Duchamp. Duchamp's photograph entitled *Trébuchet* (trap), for example, can be read as a deconstruction of the relationship between image and caption. The photograph in question pictures a coat rack. Had it been titled "coat rack," there would have been a transparent relationship between the image and the caption. As per convention and expectation, the caption would have annotated the image and the relationship between image and caption (visual and textual signifier) would have been closed—each referring to the other. As it stands, however, the apparent misalignment between the caption and the image provokes the viewer to examine the image and question why the artist thought this particular title was appropriate. Labeled as a "trap," the apparatus appears dangerous—mace-like, full of snags, something that might damage the foot if stepped on. Unconsciously one associates the metal of the rack with the skeletons of cages, animal traps, and/or barbed fishing hooks.

The word "*trébuchet*" *is a pun. When read aloud, the word is indistinguishable from the verb "trébucher,"* meaning "to trip." As recounted in an interview with Harriet Janis in 1953, a coat rack was left on the floor, where Duchamp tripped over it several times.[1] The coat rack's menacing, upward-pointing barbs worked in concert with its position on the floor to transform a benign object into something threatening. Add another meaning of "trébuchet"— to catch a king with a pawn in the game of chess.

The apparent rupture between the title and image might indicate that an industrially produced and functionally specific object, such as the coat rack, does not require a caption, especially when it is so faithfully reproduced by a photograph. The specificity of the form of the coat rack and the "objectivity" of the photographic image render the caption redundant. Being redundant, the caption is free to stray from the image to which it is tethered. The title, then, comments on its freedom as a title, and, as such, is no longer a title. This is the inverse of the phrase "in name only." The title is a title in every aspect but its name—there is more to a title than a name. A title describes a spatial as well as a semiotic relationship between a word and an image. Duchamp disrupts the latter while maintaining the former.

In a broader sense, then, the apparent lack of relation between the caption and the image comments on conventions of interpretation. Because the word "trébuchet" is positioned beneath a photograph of a coat rack the viewer assumes the two are related— that "trébuchet" is a caption for the image. There is no law, however, that insures that a word positioned beneath a given photograph refers to the photograph. This expectation is based on an unwritten law that links adjacency with thematic relation. Two things close in space are assumed to be related in content, to the extent that their juxtaposition is seen to be intentional (as it is in something framed as art). That the "title" serves the image is further reinforced by the vertical relationship between the two: things below serve things above.

An everyday object—a coat rack—is transformed by its position into something else. In a general sense this is the lesson of the Readymades: the identity of a given object is conditioned, to a large degree, by its context. This same argument, however, can be extended to the title "trébuchet," which is "trapped" into the role of title by its position with respect to the image. In turn the image (the king) is caught by the pawn, which transforms the image of a coat rack from a simple utilitarian object into a menacing and irresolvable trap.

In Duchamp's composition, the word and the image might appear, at first, to have met accidently on the page. But the presence and position of the image

transform the word "trébuchet" into a title. The frame around the composition signifies that the juxtaposition is intentional and therefore meaningful. Meaning is produced as a complex interweaving of semantic connotations with syntactic and spatial cues.

René Magritte explored the relationship between image and caption in many of his works, from the various Ceci n'est pas une pipe compositions to Personnage marchant vers l'horizon, in which words stand in for absent images. More recently the artist Gretchen Bender, in an installation at the Wexner Center for the Arts, adhered random captions onto the screens of video monitors to examine the relationship between caption and image. The apparent connection between the caption and the image was so strong and the "commentary" that these captions produced was so incisive that the viewer was shocked to discover that the video images were random local network programming. Believing the relationship to be specific, the viewer experienced it as meaningful. When intention is assumed—cued by structures such as a the frame of the video monitor (or, indeed, the art gallery)—meaning is created. Again the "intention" was to explore the spatial and conventional aspects of meaning.

René Magritte, *Personnage marchant vers l'horizon*, 1928–29

Gretchen Bender, *Aggressive Witness—Active Participant*, 1990

Robbins' work is full of similar plays with image and text. One example is what I like to call the "recreation" series, where words are arbitrarily positioned below images. The first card in this series couples a Wurlitzer organ with an image of a nail being driven through a light bulb. The word "recreation" is placed below each image. Two associations occur simul-

taneously: first, because the images are juxtaposed, one assumes they are related; second, because the word "recreation" seems a reasonable description of the function of the organ, it seems logical to associate it with the adjacent image. Under the heading of "recreation," the composition may be interpreted as contrasting the joys of public and private and/or idiosyncratic forms of entertainment.

In the second composition an image of a Thermos bottle and barbecue utensils are juxtaposed with an image of a man in a posing strap vacuuming a carpet. The words "picnic pleasures" appear beneath both images. Because "picnic pleasures" seems justifiable as a description of the left-hand image, the words are assumed to be a caption. Because the caption fits logically with the first image there is the anticipation that it should also fit the second. The elements of the composition are arranged to reinforce a relationship that is assumed to have meaning. Ambiguity exposes meaning as a relative thing—in this case, relative to the composition that casts words in the role of a caption (with respect to one image), then questions that role by positioning the words beneath an image that resists them. Either the viewer discounts the word/image relationship as absurd, or, persuaded by the structural mise-en-scène, is forced to speculate on the meaning of "pleasures" in the second image.

The artist might be thought to be comparing the experience of gustatory and sexual pleasure, or perhaps sexual as gustatory pleasure, given the relationship between the meat to be manipulated by the utensils in the first image and what is offered in the second. Or perhaps it is about the pleasures of tools: the utensils, the vacuum cleaner, and any other equipment the man might yield. Or about domesticity. The ambiguously sexual content of the vacuum cleaner and the posing strap in the right-hand image complements the ambiguous relationship between the right and left-hand images and suggests that the role of the caption might be to resolve the open-endedness—assuming, of course, that it is a caption. In the third composition an image of a coyote is coupled with an image of a bird on a tree branch—the two animals face each other across the page. The word "recreation" again appears beneath both images. While the images might be grouped under the category of "animals" and have every thematic right to appear together on a page, the word "recreation" (in its assumed role as caption) recasts the relationship in ambiguous terms. A number of interpretations suggest themselves. Whereas a wholesome, human version of recreation might be a picnic *en plein air* serenaded

Mark Robbins, *Untitled*, 1989

by the songs of birds, a coyote's idea of recreation might be to stalk and consume birds. Whereas nature is experienced as pleasurable in the first case it becomes menacing in the second. Perhaps as we are distracted by the songs of the birds the coyote stalks us. Perhaps the alarmed cries of the vigilant bird warn us that we are in danger, that the pursuit of pleasure makes us vulnerable to things that prey upon us. Perhaps in the arcadian world conjured up by the picnic, the coyote and the bird lie down with each other. Perhaps the bird is a robin, referring to the artist and alluding to his Hyde-like or lupine character. (Note that the association with picnics and the pursuit of pleasure carries over from the second composition. The fact that the three composition appear together as a series suggests that their images are thematically related.)

Perhaps the "point" in all these compositions is simply the point at which the viewer arrives, having considered a number of possible scenarios. No particular scenario seems authorized by the artist; all seem equally meaningful and meaningless. The narrative is not internal to the compositions but rather represents a dialogue in which the viewer is engaged. The ambiguous relationship between images and captions and the difficulty in deciphering the author's intentions render the viewer conscious of having

engaged in the construction of meaning. Everything about the composition suggests that its organization is intentional, and intention is interpreted as an indication of meaning. Structural cues are employed to suggest a message, yet the message is unclear. There is a kind of trespassing here, a willful misuse of conventions in order to prompt the viewer to confront expectations. In contrast to the appearance of order, the artist offers us captions that might not be captions and juxtaposes images that may or may not be related. Yet the outcome of this ambiguity is the suggestion that meaning is constructed by the viewer/interpreter when prompted by certain structural and spatial cues. The compositions question the status of meaning beyond the mechanisms that produce it and relate meaning to the desire and expectation that it be found.

The strength of this work lies in its ability to make the viewer aware of the fact that the semantic dimension of a given composition relies heavily on spatial adjacencies and framing. The ambiguity between the spatial and semantic cues suspends and relocates the question of meaning. This ambiguity throws the issue of meaning back at the viewer, who must work actively to forge it. This ambiguity also brings meaning forward as an architectural phenomenon—to the extent that the conventions that produce meaning are spatial and structural in nature, meaning has an architecture. In this sense Robbins, as an architect, is well equipped to manipulate meaning.

What is true of the relationship between image and caption in the case of Robbins' "recreation" series is also true of images. Two images placed side by side are assumed to be related. In the "mate herb" composition, an image from an advertisement found in the back of a magazine shows powder being poured into a tea cup. The powder is identified as "mate herb," an Anglicized variation on *herba mate*, a South American infusion similar to coffee or tea. The adjacent image shows a couple embracing. Through this juxtaposition the viewer is led to assume that this commonplace beverage has some

Mark Robbins, *Untitled*, 1989

aphrodisiacal power. The name "*herba mate*" (pronounced "yerba matay"), is purposefully inverted to allow it to be pronounced as if both words were English. Such a pronunciation reinforces the suggestion that the male figure is "Herb" and the woman is the "mate" he attracted.

The subtleties of this scenario are communicated subliminally. Those who encounter this composition need not know anything about *herba mate*. The juxtaposition of the images and the transposition of the name suffices to communicate what is essential. Because the images are adjacent the interpreting mind constructs a relationship. When framed, images and text signal intention and prompt the viewer to interpret them. The frame establishes relationships, which are then elaborated by alignments and adjacencies within it. The juxtaposition of images is the spatial equivalent of montage in film, where disconnected images (frames) are linked in time. The associational value of such devices are commonly exploited by printed and televised advertising.

In much of Robbins' work this association-by-adjacency is reinforced by the "architectural" frame and formal devices such as symmetry. When two images are equated across the symmetrical axis of a composition, they are assumed to be related. In *World Trade* (see p. 21), for example, a woman and a clock occupy adjacent frames in the upper right-hand corner of the composition. The characteristics of the woman recall the stereotypical "homemaker" of the late 1950s. Remembering a mother's role as timekeeper—calling us to dinner, reminding us of bedtime, etc.—the association seems plausible. In the opposite corner, however, a dog's muzzle is coupled with a drill. While the link between these elements is more difficult to construct in semantic terms, the association is reinforced by the similarity of their forms. The objects depicted are not only adjacent, similar in scale, and in similar frames, but they look alike. The viewer has the sense of being treated to a revelation—that a dog and a drill have more in common than we had ever realized. Upon reflection, however, the viewer becomes aware of having been coerced by the formal devices (symmetry and similarity of form) to make something from nothing. The dog/drill connection is experienced as a false or short-circuited logic induced by the form and position of objects. Homomorphy (the study of forms that appear similar), like adjacency (especially when reinforced by symmetry) is compelling. The human mind expects things that look alike to be related. We cannot accept form as arbitrary—we want to believe it to be the outward expression of an essential structure and meaning.

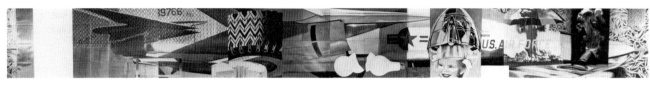

James Rosenquist, *F-111*, 1965

This play with similar forms is deployed throughout *World Trade* in increasingly persuasive ways. It suggests, for example, an affinity between the divided towers of the World Trade Center and the legs of the young man seen from behind. The phallic associations of the skyscraper are appropriate to the sexual nature of the image, although in this sense the towers refer not only to the legs but to the part of the anatomy that is hidden from view. The fact that there are two towers relates to the homoerotic content of the image—the presence of two phalli—while the separation of the towers refers again to the parted legs. Here homomorphy can be read as a trope for homosexuality—the affinity of similar things for each other. Where homomorphy is coupled with homoerotic imagery, the structure and "content" of Robbins' work begin to approach each other.

One might relate the sexual content of *World Trade* to the semantic ambiguity of the "picnic pleasures" composition: both question the obligation of the author to work within a set of time-honored conventions. When unrelated images are grouped according to the conventions of good composition (scale, symmetry, etc.), an unwritten precept has been broken. Whereas chaos has come to have its own aesthetic (as in "deconstructivism") and has been tamed in the process, the presence of compositional order is commonly taken as an indication of semantic order. Robbins' work challenges this norm in that it insists on the former but suspends the latter. It pits the compositional structure of the piece against its semantic dimension. It breaks open the question of interpretation while maintaining the frame. The apparent disjunction between the compositionally resolved structure of the piece and its open-ended meaning makes the breach of convention thematic in the work. Thus the challenge it poses is subversive—it cannot be reduced to or recognized as a style. The compositional structure of the work suggests that nothing "out of the ordinary" is going on. It is used as a rhetorical device.

The power of "association-by-adjacency" also has been explored exhaustively by Robert Rauschenberg, who elaborated the practice of collage he inherited from the cubists. Similarly, artists like James Rosenquist have used homomorphy in "stream of consciousness" compositions such as "F-111," with its implied relationship between the beauty salon dryer and the nose of the rocket. Robbins' work, while similar in spirit, departs from the work of both of these artists with respect to its use of the frame. In both his two-dimensional and three-dimensional work, the frame is everywhere present. It is against this frame (in the sense of both contrast and conflict) that the images are pitted.

The semantic ambiguity of the "recreation" series has been described as a burden placed on the viewer. The open-endedness of the work suggests that the artist or author refuses to "authorize" any particular interpretation—the author appears not to have lived up to his obligations. Furthermore, the overtly sexual imagery in much of Robbins' work represents another such breach. What is neutral with regard to birds and coyotes becomes specific when pornographic images are employed. Not only are the images "inappropriate" for framing as art, but they ridicule conventions of decency. Whereas the viewer is brought to self-consciousness when forced to construct a meaning, he or she also becomes self-conscious when exposed to pornography. Not only is it

Robert Rauschenberg, *Interview*, 1955

"inappropriate" to equate unrelated images through the use of frames, symmetry, and/or captions, but the content of such images makes them doubly inappropriate. Semantic ambiguity and sexual promiscuity unite to make the viewer self-aware. The content of the images transforms the viewer into a voyeur then keeps him locked in the role while deciphering the piece. He is literally caught in the act.

Finally, the specifically homoerotic content of the images reinforces the semantic effect of homomorphy as a structural device. It is in this respect, too, that the content is not arbitrary; that is, it becomes specific to the structure of the piece. This relationship has the effect of internalizing the reference (content to structure) and imputing an autonomy to the work. This autonomy, in turn, reinforces the composition's "right" to frame itself as art.

Theater in a Box

My comments thus far have concentrated on smaller, two-dimensional works, but the formal tendencies outlined above, as well as the links to historical antecedents in the work of Cornell and Duchamp, also apply to Robbins' three-dimensional constructions. With respect to the role of the viewer, however, Robbins departs from these influences, and his shift in emphasis is particularly evident in the three-dimensional work. Where the work of Cornell and Duchamp presupposes a static viewer, Robbins' constructions and installations often involve levels of interaction. Cornell expects the viewer to peer into the dioramas he assembles, at most shifting from foot to foot to situate components in space. A few of Duchamp's pieces demand some tactile interaction (e.g., *Box-in-a-Valise*, 1936–41), but by and large his pieces carefully locate the viewer outside the work (e.g., *Etant donnés*, 1946–66). While his work parodies the machine and includes images of things that operate, these images remain predominantly two-dimensional.

Excluding information by controlling the viewer's vantage point is a theatrical (and cinematic) device that aides in the production of illusion. Like knowledge, illusion is more often an indication of what is excluded from consideration than of what is presented. Exclusion is a function of framing: a distillation of information through editing. The viewer of

Robbins' work is often invited to transform the pieces by manipulating their frames. In this sense the frame is used rhetorically—as a malleable device whose focus and contents are constantly changing. The frame is neither neutral nor authoritative; it is the thematic red herring. It constructs a meaning that has no status beyond the frame that constructed it and that exposed itself in the process. The notion of "self-exposure" is then woven back into the piece through the use of mirrors and/or pornographic imagery. The frame becomes the looking glass through which viewers walk into their own images. And where interpretation is a physical as well as a semantic experience (as in *Night Tables* [see pp. 42–45] or the towers in *New York: Angle of Incidence* [see pp. 66–73]), the pieces make literal the idea of "constructing meaning."

Furthermore, Robbins' "theater" is not only a stage and an audience organized across the frame of a proscenium, but also a cinematic wonderland *à la* Busby Berkeley, where sets open onto a succession of others and describe a space well beyond the dimensions of the enclosure in which they are staged. Transformation—the idea of an object that, like the interpretations it sustains, changes over time—is key in the work. Whereas the works of Cornell and Duchamp constitute a kind of theater, Robbins' boxes are actively theatrical.

Busby Berkeley, still from *Wonder Bar*, 1934

Having said this, a comparison with the ideas of the physicist Schroedinger suggests itself. Schroedinger has been popularized for his illustration of the uncertainty principle. He describes a cat, enclosed in a box, being exposed to lethal radiation. To the extent that opening the box to determine whether or not the cat is alive would disrupt the experiment (perhaps killing the cat), it is impossible to know when or whether the cat has perished. According to Schroedinger the cat in the box is neither dead nor alive. Uncertainty emerges as a category of being.

The act of opening the box disrupts the relationships that the viewer perceives. In other words, the

attempt to know more about a given set of circumstances may alter the circumstances. Robbins' small constructions act as miniature stage sets into which the viewer peers. The viewer is provoked to explore the piece by noticing that components slide, hinge, etc. Manipulating these elements, however, one alters the initial set of relationships. The viewer is not neutral—to know is to alter what one knows.

While this tendency carries through the full range of Robbins' constructions and installations, a few examples may be helpful. *Triptych*, as the name suggests, is built as an operable triptych. When opened the right and left panels reveal the images of two men facing away from the center of the composition. On the left hand image is a disembodied hand; the viewer realizes that the two men are (or were) part of the same image—that the hand on the left belongs to the man on the right. The erotic implications of this point of contact come as a surprise given the overtly "masculine" demeanor of the men, which would seem to rule out any contact of a physical nature. Furthermore, it is difficult to reconstruct the relationship between the men. To the extent that we can see them at all, they are no longer touching, and to the extent that we see them fully, they are oriented away from each other. But for the hand (and the compositional symmetry that equates them) there is no indication of contact between the men. Such contact is enacted only in the darkness of the closed box.

As in *World Trade*, the compositional symmetry of the piece establishes an equivalence between the figures—an equivalence that constitutes a homology. As a compositional device, symmetry can be read as a trope for homosexuality, given its affinity for associating like with like. The operable and transformable nature of this piece, however, allows it not only to comment on the closeted nature of homoeroticism (not to mention the quasi-sacred implications of the proscribed union), but to render the viewer conscious that the information available to him is a function of his physical position and point of view. "Knowledge" (in the form of a possible scenario) is something the viewer must construct from the evidence at hand, evidence that is malleable and elusive. The viewer becomes both detective and voyeur, suspended in a state of uncertainty.

Examples of the same phenomenon occur throughout Robbins' work. In the *American Fictions* installation (see pp. 46–49), a series of screen doors line a platform. When the doors are opened to permit access to the platform, they block access along the platform—the opened doors transform the corridor

into a series of cubicles. The act of entering the space is the act of transforming the space one enters. Similarly the upper cabinet of *Two Women* (see pp. 36–37) contains a number of artifacts from the woman's life. When the box is opened the relationship between the objects is disturbed. The gears and mechanisms to which these articles are attached respond by forcing a number of the artifacts out through flaps and apertures. When one opens the box to see what is inside, nothing is there. Opening the closet sheds little light on the situation.

The closed, symmetrical states of both *Two Women* and *Triptych* suggest that there may be a particular and resolved relationship between the components to which all other states relate as transformations. The symmetry stands for this resolution. Given that this resolution corresponds to the closed state of both pieces, however, the viewer can only speculate. The spatial construction of these pieces works with the contents to assert that certain things are enacted in privacy and secrecy—whether it be a trespassing on sexual conventions or, indeed, the act of confessing such trespasses.

A Framework for Chaos?
Earlier in this essay I alluded to the "aesthetics of chaos," a topic to which it is perhaps appropriate to return when discussing Robbins' work as architecture (it is no doubt significant that up to this point I have limited my references to painters and sculptors). The last decade has seen a tendency among architects of Robbins' generation—especially those who, like Robbins, have chosen to work outside of the traditional venues of architecture—to "illustrate" chaos. From Daniel Liebiskind's *Chamberworks* to the scenographic scrolls of Wellington Reiter, there has been a tendency challenge the assumption that the architect's role is to impose a legible order on the world. Rather, the mission of these architects has been to read the "order" that exists and interpret it to and as architecture. However motivated, the work of these architects is symptomatic of a profound identity shift within a profession that is increasingly irrelevant to and marginalized within contemporary society. Whereas the postmodernists of the previous generation sought to restore order to the city and right the wrongs visited on the built environment by their modernist forbears, the present generation has had to come to terms with the possibility that there may be less at stake than they were taught to believe. Architecture has gone underground and has emerged as a counterculture. Finding itself at the margins, Robbins' generation has conceived an architecture of the marginal, of the anomaly. Its prophets have sought to recast the

terms of the endeavor, reduce the stakes, and refocus the discourse.

It is in this milieu that architectural deconstructivism has emerged—coaxed into being by the invention of the term. While the deconstructivist moment is chronologically postmodern, it can be differentiated from the forms of architectural postmodernism that immediately preceded it. Having come to terms with the relativity of history, postmodern historicism stated, in effect, that "order is artificial but we need to operate as if it weren't. " In its most informed moments it believed in the necessity of self-delusion for the presumed ultimate good of the collectivity,[2] thus while a given stance may no longer be conceptually tenable, it may be demonstrated that it is efficacious to operate "as if" it were.

Deconstructivism, on the other hand (and I impose this simple opposition to prove a point) states that "order is artificial; therefore we must attack it and/or replace it." While more often than not the resulting architecture is predicated on negation—whether the negation of platonic form, gravity, stasis or, indeed, the (conceptual or structural) frame—this position is as optimistic as it is nihilistic. In good dialectic fashion, the violence it directs against "the orders that be" opens the way for a new order. As implied by its name, deconstructivism goes both ways. By eliding literary deconstruction with Russian constructivism it appropriates deconstruction for its use in a historical struggle for developmental self-expression. This struggle is fundamentally modern in its goals and assumptions: the struggle is utopian and its assumptions positivistic. It believes in the possibility of a new metaphor to reinstate architecture's relationship to truth, similar to the way in which chaos theory attempts to reinstate science's claim to ultimate authority by extending its purview beyond the narrow limits of Newtonian physics. Deconstructivism is positivistic in the sense that it believes in a correct fit between form and culture. Thus, compared to its historicist predecessor, deconstructivism is a kind of fundamentalism tied to the possibility of and therefore the imperative of truth.[3]

This essay offers the work of Mark Robbins as an informed middle ground between these two positions. Whereas his contemporaries revel in the absence of the frame (indisputably a relevant and visually compelling stance), Robbins insists upon its presence. It is the difference between saying "it might not be true but it is necessary and useful" (postmodern historicism),[4] "it isn't true therefore let's abandon it" (deconstructivism),[5] and saying "there isn't a truth but the notion is certainly useful, therefore let's ex-

plore its constructability." This latter position, the one that I attribute to Robbins, locates the problem not in the validity of the frame with respect to truth, but in the viewer's need to construct the world according to such devices. Whereas deconstructivism abandons or physically attacks the frame, Robbins' work undermines the frame (and by implication the role of framing) with what is framed. In the case of deconstructivism, the frame is literally undone, whereas in Robbins' constructions it is semantically disassembled. In deconstructivism all discourse is stopped, precisely because it is not legibly framed, unless, or course, the work is set against a relatively stable and traditional architectural context.[6] Without the frame it becomes *merely* stylistic.

One might argue that it is only against such a frame that deconstructivism can effectively operate (i.e., become anything other than a stylistic investigation), in which case it is strangely dependent on the historicist position it decries. To the extent that historicists (e.g., Ricardo Bofil) devalue the "real" historical context (pre-World War II urbanism), they undermine the deconstuctivist's position. This, however, places deconstructivism squarely in the context of "traditional" urban sites and ideologies and suggests that it has little to say, add, or contribute to the context of the suburban city of the last fifty years. In this sense, again, the movement might appear surprisingly reactionary, although it is impossible to tell until the first few deconstructivist car showrooms are built at highway interchanges. One assumes that the context alone will be enough to "re-frame" the discourse. Whereas the deconstructive project, to the extent that it may be characterized as a project, is more a question of providing a reading of the context than reacting to it. The "ism" of "deconstructivism" places it in the ambiguous, agenda-laden, and stylistically circumscribed circumstances in which it is addressed here.

In Robbins' work the frame is rhetorical: it is both there (physically) and not there (semantically). It is not a culprit but a conspirator—a catalyst that engenders meaning and, in turn, is destabilized by it. In this respect Robbins' work does not privilege the symptom over the problem. His constructions differentiate between destabilized meaning and destabilized form—the very equation that deconstructivists all too easily make. Because his work is not primarily about form it cannot be reduced to a style, a "look." By diverting the issue from form he not only turns his back on the stylistic preoccupations of the history of architecture, but on the deconstructivist project as well. His work is neither ideological in the terms of deconstructivism nor in terms of postmod-

ern historicism. While inviting interpretation and availing itself of all of the classical cues and indications it does not prescribe or reduce interpretation. It undermines the question of order from the inside, leaving it both intact and open-ended.

While Robbins' work may be considered "traditional" by the standards of composition in contemporary architecture, it is aggressive in its exploration of meaning. The play of juxtaposition, homomorphy and captions within an apparently stable framework heightens the disjunction between expectation and "reality." Where deconstructivists such as Coop Himmelblau play their hyper-animated forms against the framework of nineteenth-century Vienna, Robbins constructs both the framework and the commentary. The point is not to show that all frames can be avoided, distorted, or subverted, but to reveal the role of the frame in the construction of meaning. In Robbins' constructions the frame is both used and "unmasked," bringing the viewer to an awareness that meaning is something that is constructed according to syntactical and formal cues.

1. Anne d'Harnancourt, *Marcel Duchamp* (New York: Prestel/Museum of Modern Art, 1989), 283.
2. Though one should be careful to distinguish its benign, self-conscious forms as represented by Robert A. M. Stern and Michael Graves, etc., and its rabid, self-righteous forms as represented by Leon Krier and Prince Charles.
3. I am aware that I am letting postmodern historicism off the hook too easily. More often than not the rhetoric that surrounded this ideology was the rhetoric of "right versus wrong," the rhetoric which still characterizes Prince Charles' take on the situation. Postmodern historicism can be easily more reactionary than the most motivated forms of deconstructivism. The question is always the rhetorical intention behind the work, which is an indication of how self-conscious the orator is of his or her position. The degree of humor in the work is usually an indication of the degree of self-consciousness. While I a m not by any means advocating his architecture, Charles Moore is an example of a postmodern historicist who "knew the score."
4. Or indeed: "because it is useful it must be true."
5. Which assumes that, as noted above, that there is a truth against which the falsity of the former systems of order might be judged.
6. Take, for example, Peter Eisenman's Wexner Center framed against the two pre-existing auditoria, or Coop-Himmelblau's Attic Conversion, 1984–88, framed against the cornices of the nineteenth-century fabric of Vienna (see Papadakis et al., eds., *Deconstructivism: Omnibus Volume* [New York: Rizzoli, 1989], 225.)

The Building That Looks Back
P. A. Morton

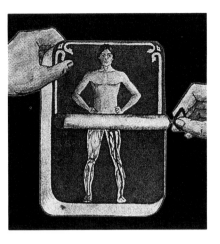

One day, I was on a small boat, with a few people from a family of fishermen in a small port . . . [A]s we were waiting for the moment to pull in the nets, an individual known as Petit-Jean . . . pointed out to me something floating on the surface of the waves. It was a small can, a sardine can. It floated there in the sun, a witness to the canning industry, which we, in fact, were supposed to supply. It glittered in the sun. And Petit-Jean said to me—*You see that can? Do you see it? Well, it doesn't see you.*[1]

Mark Robbins and Benjamin Gianni describe their installation "American Fictions" in terms of "buildings that have eyes and return stares," in other words, buildings that look back. Robbins has made the relation among object, subject, and gaze—and the otherness of the gaze—one of his architectural investigations. The notion of designing buildings that return the look of the viewer and "embody the gaze," in Robbins and Gianni's words, makes viewing and observation the point of the architectural investigation. In Robbins' architecture, the implicit link between the gaze and the object is made explicit by the building.

In the Lacanian theory of the gaze, the object is already gazing at one when one looks at it—the sardine can is looking back at you. The eye viewing the object is on the side of the subject, while the gaze is on the side of the object. This means that the gaze always comes from the field of the Other. Sartre puts it in a slightly different way when he says that "my fundamental connection with the Other-as-subject must be able to be referred back to my permanent possibility of *being seen* by the Other." This permanent possibility means that "a subject who sees me may be substituted for the object seen by me."[2]

Windows and frames are the most direct incarnation of the gaze. Windows carry connotations of eyes, of the stare of the unseeable observer behind the glass. This observer is analogous to the watcher in Bentham's Panopticon, in which the inmates can never be sure whether they are under surveillance. Sartre uses the analogy of a farmhouse seen by men during an attack: the men apprehend the farmhouse as a "look to be avoided." As the support for the gaze, the eye is the farmhouse; the window and the farmhouse represent the eye to be feared, not the literal eye of someone watching behind the window.

Although the window implies transparency, congruity between inside and outside, and a democratic visibility of everything on both sides, it acts as a mirror or a black hole according to the presence or absence of light. Windows materialize the threshold between inside and outside and the boundary between the different experiences of each side. The frame can both clarify and obfuscate objects and bodies. It can bring things into focus by concentrating attention on them and can simultaneously conceal things that are not revealed within the aperture. The mystery of things that are not visible is the threat contained in the window and the frame.

There is another sense in which Robbins' architecture looks back: by referring to other spaces and forms that constitute the city and by their appropriation and re-presentation. Images taken from the realm of the familiar and repositioned are still legible, but they elicit diverse responses from the viewers, depending on their experiences. The building "looks back" by means of images and forms that Robbins pilfers from various contexts and makes them available for the viewer's interpretation. Robbins makes the ordinary strange in order to invoke reactions that are not limited by the ostensible "meaning" of the pirated object.

Consistent with Lacan's logic, Robbins' buildings look at the viewer in terms of the antinomic relationship between the gaze and the eye. They do not employ nostalgia, in which this antinomy is concealed through fascination with a domesticated gaze of the Other, which allows us to imagine that we "see ourselves seeing." Instead, the building acts like the gaze, as a "blot" that obscures the transparency of the viewed image, such that we cannot see the point at which it gazes back at us and the incommensurability of the eye and the gaze (myself and the object) is retained.[3]

Further, this architecture requires the anamorphic gaze, "looking awry" in Slavoj Zizek's words, the sidelong glance that sees the anamorphically distorted representation as a clear image. Robbins' allusions and borrowings can be read directly, but they reveal themselves most completely from the side, from the margins, as the manifestation of myriad types of stimuli. The referents are not self-evident although they seem familiar. Some of the images and spaces are personal icons while others are generic figures, such as a dog, which he uses for their general allusive power. The spatial forms of the stalls of "Framing American Cities" might be telephone booths, changing rooms, confessionals, or toilet stalls. The ambiguous quality of the architectural forms allows for various readings of the allusions, but the richest are those that come from the range of urban life found in these ubiquitous cubicles.

Robbins explores the relationship between the city and the body as an intrinsic part of the urban experience by using windows and openings in the installations and frames in the boxes and other pieces to isolate parts of the body. The body is fragmented, dissected, and objectified—its parts presented to the look of other viewers. Robbins heightens the association of the body with architecture by frequently including a male body, often nude, in his work. The buildings that look back, therefore, double their viewing function by the presence of the seeing body. The status of the body and that of the gaze become more complex in this visual economy.

Robbins creates a specific relationship in which the body is not just the creator of the city, but its correlate; the body and the city produce each other and are inextricably intertwined together. In her article, "Bodies-Cities,"[4] Elizabeth Grosz posits a relationship between the body and the city that is neither causal nor representational, but rather one of "interface," a two-way linkage between complex assemblages of parts. This system is not unified or monolithic; it is contingent and temporary. According to her formulation, "the city is made and made over into the simulacrum of the body, and the body, in its turn, is transformed, 'citified,' urbanized as a distinctively metropolitan body." The body is an amorphous, incomplete entity that acquires formation through the social and built environment, the city.

Robbins' inclusion of bodies in his projects can be read through this affiliation between body and city, particularly in "New York: Angles of Incidence," a section of "Framing American Cities." Robbins establishes the symbiotic relationship between the body and the city by making constructions that require the physical body in order to be read and to be complete. As a body passes in front of an electric eye, it activates video screens and audio equipment positioned on a platform with towers. The towers must be manipulated by embracing them. The windows between the cubicles can only be operated by two people cooperating in sliding them up and down. The frames and windows highlight fragments of the viewers' bodies (as in all of Robbins' pieces), which can be seen from the scopophilic viewing positions (bleachers, "curtain wall," platform) he establishes within the installation.

The "interface" between body and city is contained within the spaces to which Robbins refers, the places for the control or social administration of the body. The shower stall, urinal, toilet, and examination room, along with the office cubicle, waiting

room, voting booth, and cell are the public spaces of the body's control. As Grosz puts it:

> As a hinge between the population and the individual, the body, its distribution, habits, alignments, pleasures, norms, and ideals are the ostensible object of governmental regulation, and the city is a key tool.[5]

Through reference to the spaces of regulation, Robbins creates a simulated city of ordinance. The bodies of the spectators constitute the physical material on which the city works and the concomitant site that produces the city. Whereas architecture is traditionally exclusively concerned with the city and the regulation of bodies, Robbins makes explicit the interdependency of architecture and the body.

Robbins further investigates the body in the city as the point at which the politics of the body's sexual formation (by the city) becomes explicit. The male body signifies sexuality differently than the female body (which is sexualized in heterosexual visual norms). The nude male body is visually coded as the "scale-figure" of architectural representation, the "Vitruvian Man" encapsulated by architectural proportion. It signifies the celebration of the male body in gay culture, and it is the object of the viewer's gaze, equivalent to the building.

By making the male body the object of the gaze, Robbins causes a disruption of the "normal" sexual economy of the gaze. As theorized by Laura Mulvey and other feminist film theorists, the gaze operates from male subject to female object, from the man as bearer of the look to the woman as image. This relationship is established in heterosexual terms, but can be subverted by making the male the spectacle, the erotic object, and by introducing a female spectator.

According to the principles of the ruling ideology and the physical structures that back it up, the male figure cannot bear the burden of sexual objectification. Man is reluctant to gaze at his exhibitionist like.[6]

Richard Dyer counters this when he says that images of men produce in him an oscillation between identification and desire. Dyer maintains that representations of men are necessary to the formation of the gay male self image as a part of the way in which they positively identify themselves. The "exhibitionist-like" male body originates a sense of connection with the image, an image that Dyer claims is read as "different than woman."[7]

The male nude body, as Robbins uses it, is not just the neutral "scale figure" or classical human referent

for the building, but the sexually coded body as it is constructed in the city. The framing and fragmentation of the male body into isolated parts in a shallow, theatrical space focuses the spectator's attention on the sexual affinity of these bodies. In other words, they can be read as the bodies of gay men, although the deliberate complexity of associations carried by the forms sponsors an ambiguity of interpretation. The dual traditions of the classical male nude and the pin-up make a counterpoint to the displaced forms and spaces of Robbins' borrowings that eludes easy categorization or facile explanation.

The modes in which Robbins' buildings "look back" conspire to create a complex referential architecture. They operate within the scopic realm as objects with eyes that return the look and embody the gaze through ordinary architectural elements—windows and frames, most importantly—that carry the potential for voyeurism and surveillance. In the translation of urban forms in his installations, Robbins uses as referent the material of city life as experienced by the policed body. This is accomplished when Robbins repositions and transforms spaces and images from the city and juxtaposes male bodies to architectural forms. The interdependency of city and body, and of viewer and object, is made into a theme by his work such that the norms of viewing are undermined at that moment when the building "looks back."

1. Jacques Lacan, *The Four Fundamental Concepts of Psychoanalysis* (New York: Norton, 1981), 95.
2. Jean-Paul Sartre, *Being and Nothingness* (New York: Washington Square Press, 1966), 344.
3. Slavoj Zizek, *Looking Awry: An Introduction to Jacques Lacan through Popular Culture* (Cambridge, MA: MIT Press, 1991), 114.
4. Elizabeth Grosz, "Bodies-Cities," in *Sexuality and Space*, ed. Beatriz Colomina (New York: Princeton Architectural Press, 1992), 241–253.
5. Grosz, Bodies, 249.
6. Laura Mulvey, "Visual Pleasure and Narrative Cinema," in *Feminism and Film Theory* (New York and London: Routledge, 1988) 63. By "man," I take it that Mulvey means "heterosexual man."
7. Richard Dyer, "A Conversation about Pornography," in *Coming on Strong*, ed. Simon Shepard and Mick Wallis (London: Unwin Hyman, 1989), 202.

Projects

World Trade

In this collage the towers of the World Trade Center are split and repositioned on either side of two male figures. Small images of the home and workplace from a farm implement catalogue are placed above these panels.

1980, collage
Postcard, acetate

Triptych

A secular scene of American life ca. 1952 is inserted within the frame of a postcard of an ivory reliquary. Its side panels, with bas-relief angels, are reversed and hinged as doors, which open onto a small niche. Beneath the Gothic trefoil, the portal of the Washington Square Arch opens out to the space of a city. The inside faces of the doors are backed with images from *National Geographic* of two teenage campers at a dude ranch. Above images of mom and a porter, two comrades from WWI hover together in the tympanum. Under the street, a panel with an advertisement for an engine opens onto a facade made up of letters taken from the stock pages. A woman's eyes and mouth, fragments of a Valentine's Day card, are applied below.

1980, construction
Chipboard, postcard

Syracuse Box

A cycle of the history of the city of Syracuse, New York is represented in a doubly hinged box. Each exterior facade depicts aspects of the life of the town. Two sets of doors open onto cross sections of subterranean rooms and framed shadow boxes. When the piece is fully opened, a narrative line can be read between panels of historic scenes, corporate logos, and domestic settings.

1980, construction
Chipboard, mirror, found images, plasteline

Italian Tower

This construction was made
to be viewed on four sides
and supports views of theatrical stage-set conventions.
A concentric rectilinear
structure frames perspec-
tival views. Floating saints
and hidden nudes by Giulio
Romano become visible as
the piece is rotated.

1981, construction
Chipboard, found images

City Altars

Just north of Times Square a municipal parking structure lets out ten small showcase windows, for the lack of a paying advertiser, to art groups. I asked seven other architects in New York—Brian McGrath, Deborah Gans, Neil Denari, Jude LeBlanc, Sophia Gruzdys, and Mary Pepchinski—to fill one or two of these small spaces. This project, given the title City Altars, was shown during Christmas.

My own window housed a diorama with a structure, loosely based, on Raphael's School of Athens. The project was a triptych with a composite of buildings from several American cities occupying the center. Behind these grand urban silhouettes a series of wooden shacks could be seen in the reflection in the mirrored backdrop. To the left of this scene was a three-part assemblage of classical statuary and Platonic solids. Opposite this, cutouts from a fifth-grade class picture (ca. 1965, Queens, New York) filled the panel. The middle ground of the panel was occupied by the form of a suburban house apparently sinking into the ground above flash cards of competing wildlife. Mirrored side chapels revealed images not visible to the frontal view of the passersby. The materiality of the paper and painted wood construction was of a (humanist) piñata, a gilt shrine on the street.

1983, installation
Cardboard, clay, found images
10 on 8 Windows, New York, New York

10 on 8 Windows
8th Avenue and 53rd Street

Images of rural America are presented in the heightened context of a reliquary; Urbino meets Port Arthur. On the white-washed front facade a lead and linoleum inlay implies the perspectival depth of a room. The actual interior and its contents can be seen through a series of slats at the back of the piece. The thick doors open to reveal two plaster bas-relief cows encased in green painted wood frames. In the center a mirrored panel can be pulled down, like an attic stair, to expose a bright red flight of stairs, which terminate on a small centrally placed frame. This might be the image of a child's view at the top of the stairs looking out of the house.

1986, construction
Basswood, lead, linoleum, glass, steel grate, copper, mirror

A green painted box opens
onto a partitioned photo-
graph and diorama of a
nineteenth-century Hippo-
drome building in Argentina,
its architecture encrusted
with decorative lattice and
ironwork. From the top of
the box an insert slides up-
ward, exposing a lead-lined
cubicle with a barred opening. This space can be read
as a cellular room seen
from the inside with its view
blocked by grating. The op-
posing panel in the diptych
can be read as the spatial
inverse; it places the viewer
on the outside viewing
through the grid of a fence
to the inaccessible colonial
structure. Successive
stages of unfolding hinged
and sliding partitions transform the symmetrical and
closed object, revealing discordant interior conditions.

1986, construction
Basswood, lead, glass,
postcard

Terminal Box

This box was shown in a room at the Brooklyn Marine Terminal, a building that served as the embarkation point for troops headed overseas during WWII. Within this small cabinet is an image from *LIFE* magazine of men aboard ship. The tinted image has been turned, upending the three litters, and placed behind window screening. The inside of the lead-covered doors are lined with torn cotton and satin, with a tag of the Lords Prayer stamped on a penny. On the side of the box a movie still is framed and set behind glass. It is a promotional shot from *Since You Went Away* with Robert Taylor and Jennifer Jones.

1983, construction
Lead, cotton, wood, gold
and silver leaf, linoleum

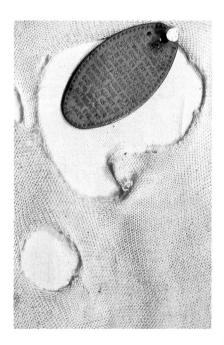

Two American friends with tumbleweed on the western horizon are on one side; Greek classical heads and the American classicism of Eakins figures are on the other.

1983, construction
Postcard, found images, 35mm transparency, film leader

Room in the City

A 400-square-foot apartment (fig. a) at the top floor of a seven-story walk-up in New York's Little Italy was the site for this project. It was one of nine proposals for the design of apartments in a single tenement in the exhibition "Room in the City."

The new plan (fig. b) is divided into two equal parts. In the rear half, facing the air shaft, the elements of domestic activity are densely packed. The sleeping/working room with bed and armoire/desk and the hall dining room with its mobile table/chair sit on either side of two glass-enclosed cubicles, which contain bath and kitchen, at the center. The other half of the apartment is given over to an open living space.

The central wall divides public from private, setting up the dominant visual axes. From within the small rooms, views are framed toward the exterior windows out over the urban landscape of the city. In the living space, direct views into the apartment are framed like still-life compositions. The lateral glance, from within the dense cluster of rooms, skewers the three spaces though steam and diffused glass, from bed to bath.

1987, model
Basswood, poplar pine, gilding

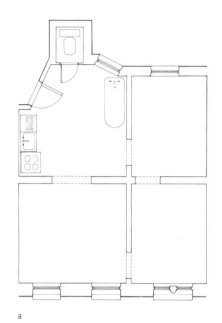

a

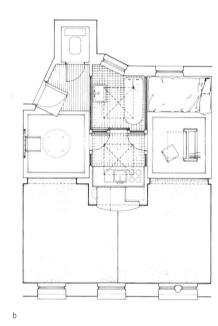

b

Guest Chair

This project was one of a collection of furniture made from salvage and shown in an unused storefront in a subterranean concourse in Grand Central Station. The found chair's seat was replaced with a layer of steel grate bolted to a 3/4-inch Plexiglas panel. A pivoting mirror was suspended below this on rigid metal straps. In the place of an arm a vertical post was attached to the side chair. At the top of this post a small revolving mirror was positioned at the eye level of a seated person.

The chair is imagined in use, perhaps as multiples, for a dinner of six or eight around a formal table set with draping cloth. The chairs face inward to the audience around the table, like facades of summer cottages toward the open ellipse of a lake. In the hand mirror, each speaker, venturing a *bon mot* or indiscretion, sees his or her own face at the same time as the face of the person being addressed. Which to look at? From behind the seats, the help, the hostess, or your new pal can observe the hidden scene below in the mirror, the play of feet below the voluble table of guests.

1988, assemblage
Mirror, Plexiglas, copper tubing, steel grate, found chair

Two Women

A young woman living in Connecticut commissioned this biographical piece. She races yachts and edits television news. The piece is configured in two parts: a wooden cabinet and a supporting armature of solid stainless steel. The door to the upper part, which is covered in calfhide with zinc flashing, is connected to a rack.

As the cabinet is opened, this rack drives a set of gears. A gridded form, conceived as a sail, is propelled through the interior of the cabinet. This gear mechanism causes copper plates, etched with images from the owner's childhood, to spin around the central axle. The smallest of these is a picture of the subject as a young girl in a velvet skating dress pirouetting on the ice. The larger one shows brothers and sisters on the back of a mule in front of the family house on a tidal estuary of Long Island Sound. When the door to the cabinet is closed a green plumb bob resets a small panel in the side of the case, resealing it.

The relationship between the dark hide and the smooth white wood on the front of the piece is reversed on the back. This change in material reinforces the seam that runs throughout the piece, encouraging a reading of it as two towers that remain separate entities while touching; the two women. The motion of opening the door drives the sail through the hollow cavity linking both towers internally. Below the wooden chamber, within the stainless steel framework, a cast bronze of the woman's upper torso spans the two towers. It is an ambiguous terrain of land or water or body, obscured behind panes of irregular glass.

1986–90, construction
Stainless steel, bronze, maple veneer plywood, glass, calfhide

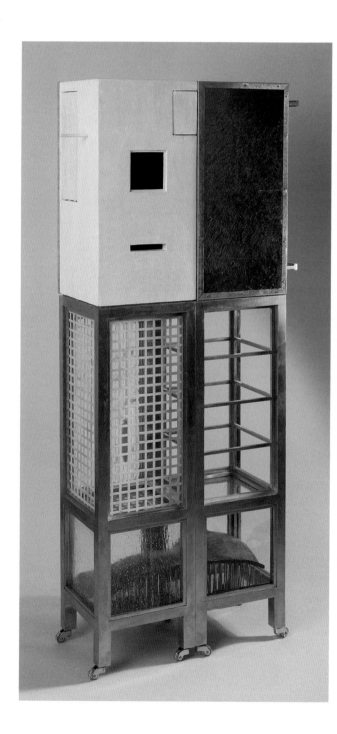

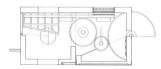
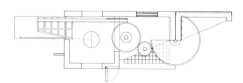
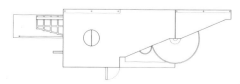

Utopian Prospect

Built during a summer residency, the piece is located at the Byrdcliffe Art Colony, a failed utopian community founded in 1902 by Ralph Whitehead, a student of Ruskin. Today the grounds comprise a six-hundred-acre preserve with arts-and-crafts style cottages and overgrown ruins of formal gardens, building foundations, and brick chimney stacks. The installation is sited on a bluff that lies between the remains of the colony and the vistas of the rounded hills of the Catskill range. Its placement suggests two concepts of Utopia, one achieved through rational construction, the other through reconciliation with the natural world.

Utopian Prospect is composed of two major elements: a wall and a pier. The smooth side of the block wall supports a steel shutter, which can be pivoted by hand into positions that either mask or frame views through a large window at eye level. On this side of the wall a flight of

stairs descends into a cool recess in the earth. It provides access to views through a smaller window. This window is located two feet above the ground on the reverse side of the wall, which has the rough texture of split-faced block, suggesting an exterior condition. Here a bleached wood bench offers unobstructed views out over the landscape. The wall sponsors interaction between viewers or provides a barrier, allowing for solitude.

On the brick pier, a metal rod with a frame at either end spins on bearings in the wind. As it moves the mirrored frame reflects, alternately, the forest and the brown weathered cottages. It inscribes the view from behind into the landscape ahead of the viewer.

1988, installation
Split-faced block, bluestone, mild steel, mirror, colored glass
Byrdcliffe Colony, Woodstock, New York

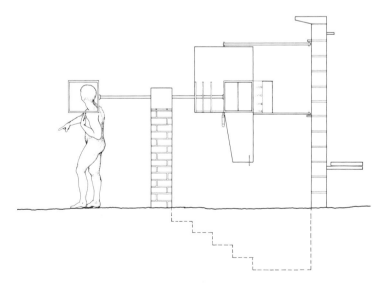

Eisenstein setting up a shot for *Staroye i Novoye [Old and New]*

Night Tables

At a scale suggesting furniture, *Night Tables* are a series of studies with weights and mirrors. The pieces explore the relationship between irregular, organic materials and machined or orthogonal systems. The body- and gender-allusive symbols are juxtaposed with rigidly structured frameworks, whose architecture is suggestive of animal or human forms.

One set of the pieces has a mirrored top surfaces with a square of silvering scraped away to offer a view inside. Each has paired hinges located on opposite sides of its basswood frames, allowing it to unfold in two directions like a road map. A reclining nude, a copper panel, and a small window are uncovered.

The second set of frames opens onto lead- or calfhide-lined spaces. These are held in position out of plumb by weights caught in metal grates.

1987–89, construction
Lead, basswood, calfhide, mirror

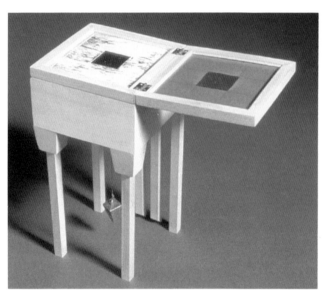

Night Table I

Sheraton; lady's work table

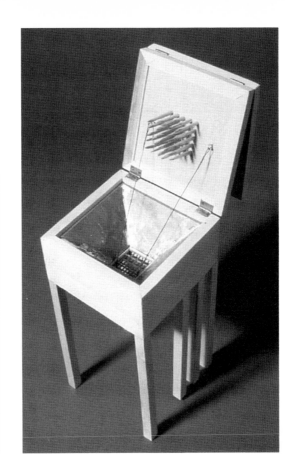

Night Table II

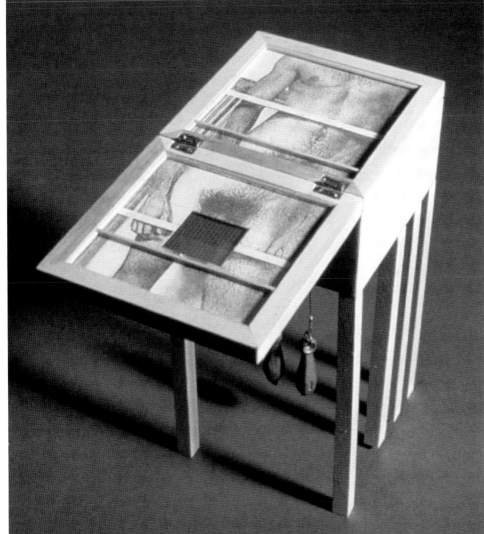

Night Table III

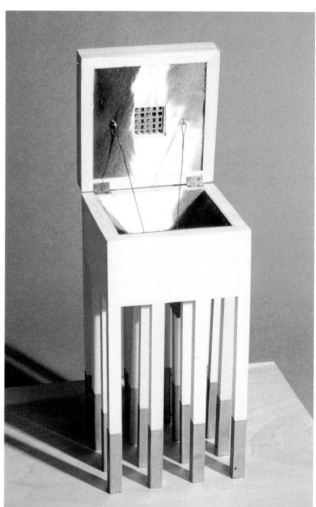

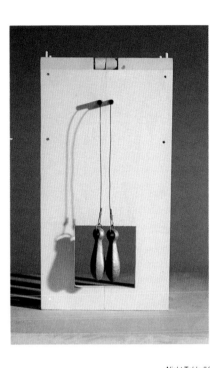

Night Table IV

American Fictions

with Benjamin Gianni

This installation was made up of two parallel walls: one a canvas hung from the ceiling, the other an exposed wooden frame anchored to large risers. Set into the frames, a series of screen doors opened into the space between the two walls to form a succession of cubicles. From this space, *Night Tables*, small movable constructions, could be viewed. Openings in the bronzed canvas provided views across the gallery towards etchings of rural buildings on desolate landscapes. The field of the frame in each case was at odds with the specific objects seen.

American Fictions evoked the spatial conditions of U.S. cities and towns in the narrow space of a gallery positioning both viewers and objects. The canvas wall—with its spiky, metallic, skin—operated as an urban facade, creating a complex proscenium for figures that moved in and out of view through its screened openings. The apertures were positioned to isolate various parts of the viewers' bodies. The frame wall, of standard 2x4inch construction and rural in character, served as a spatial foil, with its layers of screens. The space between these two planes provided an ambiguous stage for viewing and being viewed—as benign as a porch, as intimate as a changing booth.

1989, installation
Wood, canvas, screen doors, rubber matts
John Nichols Gallery,
New York, New York

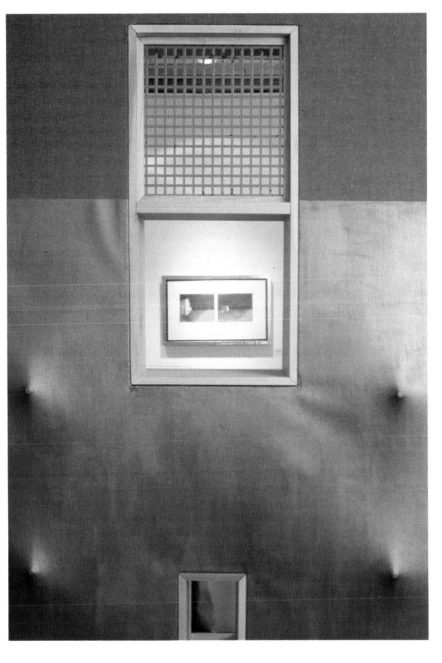

Pompeii Studies

This series of gouaches and small panel paintings were completed upon return from studying wall frescoes in Pompeii, Herculaneum, and environs. They use conventions of perspective representation to suggest depth and overlapping of planes.

1989, painting
Gouache on chipboard

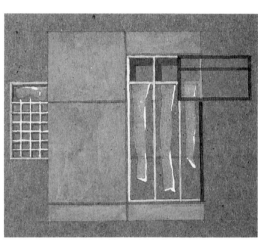

House of the Vettii, Pompeii

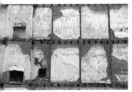

Urban ruins, New York

Cast of man, sleeping dog, Pompeii

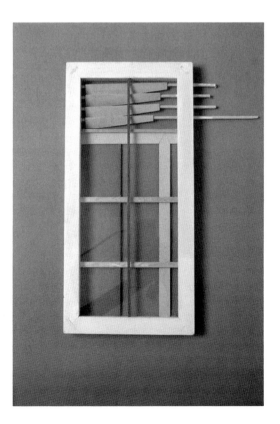

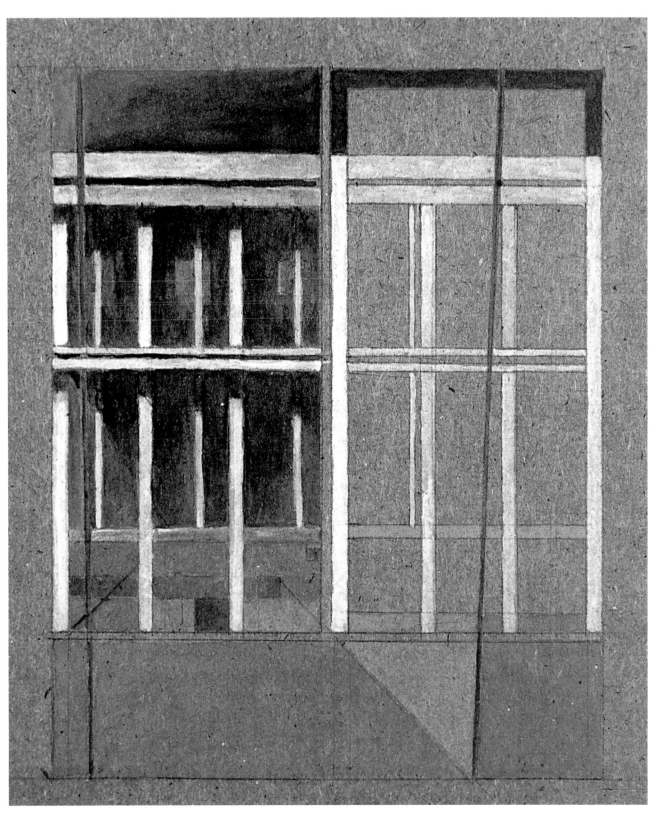

Lolita I
Lolita II

The image of Sue Lyons is
taken from an ad for Stanley
Kubric's film of Vladimir
Nabokov's *Lolita*. The depiction of the juvenile odalisque
is overlaid with planes that
indicate the deep space of
landscapes as well as clinical fragments of male anatomy. These are preparatory
sketches for the *Winesburg*
project.

1989, collage
Gouache, photocopies

Winesburg I
Winesburg II

with Benjamin Gianni

A story from Sherwood Anderson's *Winesburg, Ohio*, was used as the starting point for this project, which attempted to embody a narrative specific to the Midwest. The story selected, "The Strength of God," involves a minister's longing for a young school teacher he spies through a hole in the leaded glass of the church bell tower in which he prepares his sermons. Through the leaded glass image of Christ with little children, he sees her bare neck and shoulders as she smokes cigarettes on her bed. The story tracks his struggle with desire for the unknowing object.

The story and its architectural setting expressed for us the problem of perspective; the interpretation of the events peculiar to each character reveals the interrelationship of physical and psychological points of view. Our project derived its form in part from abstractions of spatial relationships and building types described in the text: the clapboard facade, the window, the tower, etc. An engraving of the Quadratura Table, Dürer's perspective construction device, also suggested appropriate forms in which to illustrate the power of the male gaze. The grid of the quadratura, the leaded glass, and the Midwestern plat mesh in the

minister's tower piece. It is a combination pulpit and viewing device, incorporating a suspended interior cabinet that sways. The cabinet is composed of a series of louvers onto which fractured images of the male body are applied. The tower is positioned opposite the billboard-like structure that represents the realm of the house. A single window cut into the facade makes visible a perspectival bed. An odalisque, in the image of a popular nineteenth-century American *Maja*, is pasted on this facade. The clapboarded surface of this billboard hinges open as a series of slats, intercutting the interior realm of the inhabitant with the interior as the voyeur imagines it.

While the first construction proposed two separate structures to represent the minister and the maiden, the second sketch model connected these into one kinetic piece. In it each vertical frame is on wheels and supports a horizontal trough. There are elements suggesting a lectern, a viewing device, a scourge, and a grain sower. Formally there are projections and voids that seem to suggest a possible union. But as each piece rolls toward the other the entire construction is destabilized, eventually collapsing on its narrow supports.

1989, model
Basswood

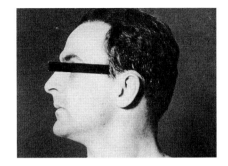

Female subject

Male subject

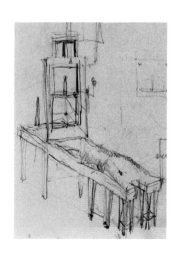

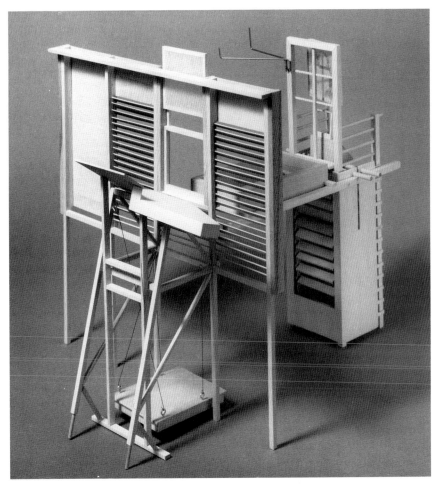

Left and facing page: Winesburg I
Below: Winesburg II

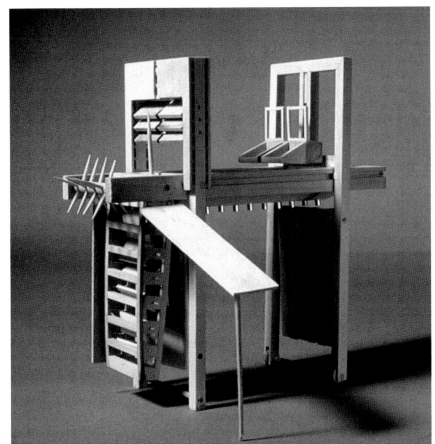

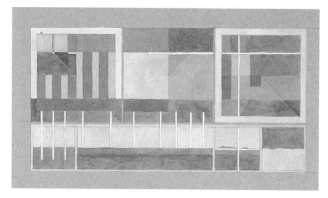
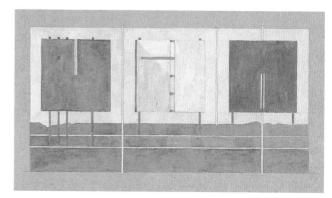
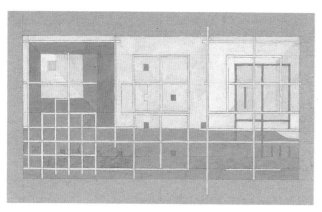
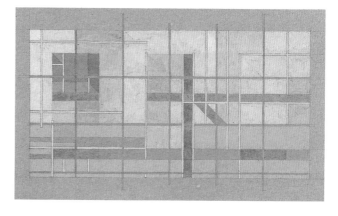

1990, painting
Gouache on chipboard

Veiled Men

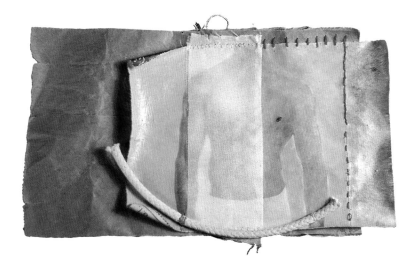

Both collages are assembled with thread and cover the figure with silk; one is slick and the other raw and unattractive. A fetishized young torso from a Chelsea Gym advertisement is contrasted with a washed-out image of a self-photographed man. In the second photo the man's eyes have been blanked out, as in clinical studies or taxonomies of criminal types; his identity is hidden from his activity. A screen of pine twigs further obscures the figure. The twigs are hung like ermine tails on a French royal robe and tied to the veil with blue thread in a quincunx pattern.

1990, collage
Silk, twigs, thread, rope, gouache on newsprint, magazine images

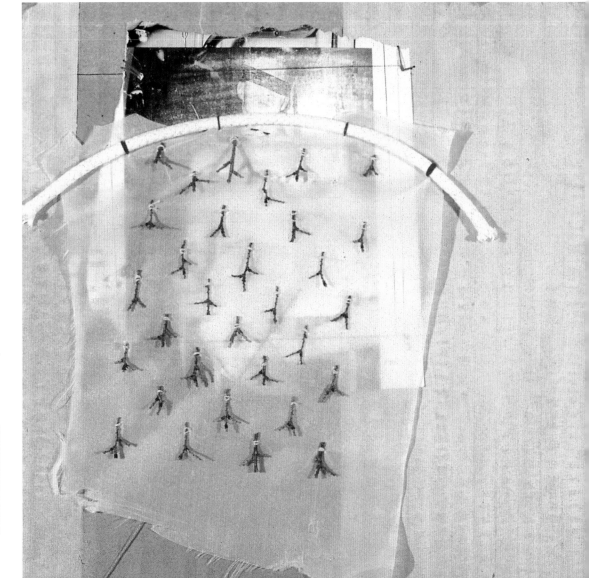

Signs and Wonders

with Benjamin Gianni

For this temporary installation in Pittsburgh two residents of the industrial city were selected as twin armatures for the project: evangelist Kathryn Kuhlman and artist Andy Warhol. The two subjects share a similar set of aspirations and methods. Both elevated the pitch over the content of their sale and manipulated mass media, making use of a ready-made system of signs and symbols. Both aspired to a transcendence enacted through the media itself. Kuhlman's stage, as witnessed by her audience and the TV eye, was the scene of her own apotheosis, "living" proof of her message and spiritual incarnation. Warhol and his artifacts, films, prints, and publications operated in a similar fashion. The media provide the vehicle and the context for notoriety, the ultimate approbation available to the human being.

We posited Warhol as a witness in attendance at one of Kuhlman's miracle services. The image of the stage was transformed into a structure that was both sanctuary and gallery. It rested on legs of rubber-tipped crutches, propping the structure's single raised aisle. This was shielded by

two screens, one of wooden slats and springs, the other a series of black frames holding asphalt shingles on one side, mirrors on the other. The large nylon tricot panel represented Kuhlman, suspended above the audience; a sheer, tightly stretched panel connected by red fishing lines and hooks to the mirrored panels. These move to a random computer-generated pulse as the broadcast voice of the evangelist demands a miracle on the remixed tape loop in the gallery.

The screens set up multiple frames, turning the gallery visitor into a participant—both image and audience. The structure insists that the visitor be an active messenger bearing a combination of Warhol's and/or Kuhlman's missals. Through its diagonal positioning in a narrow space *Signs and Wonders* forces the viewer's gaze through a series of reflective panels and the translucent scrims of the evangelist, in search of new signs.

1991, installation
Wood, nylon, tar paper, shingle, mirror
Hewlitt Gallery, Carnegie-Mellon University, Pittsburgh, Pennsylvania

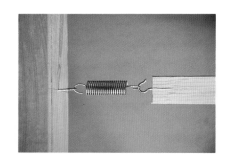

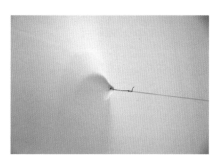

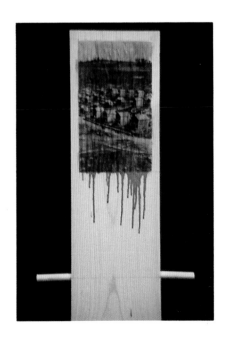

Departmental Chair

The piece is situated between rooms used by staff, administration, and faculty and has a cushioned bench as its center. The occupant of the upholstered window seat is visible through a framed opening opposite the clerical staff and the chair's office. Depending on the seat's use it is either a place to wait, to observe, or to command the conference room.

Departmental Chair takes the form of three partitions: a sliding pocket-door, a Sheetrock panel with window and seat, and a grid of moving panels holding mirrors on one side and cork on the other. The central panel appears as an object from inside the conference room, and, with the door retracted, as a more neutral wall from the exterior. As the louvered pocket-door is closed the window in the Sheetrock wall is cleared of the obstructing panel, permitting a view of the inhabitants of the room behind. This door is also the mechanism that controls the position of the panels on the third leaf of the triptych. As the door is pulled the panels spin, alternately flashing mirror and random messages pinned to the cork surfaces.

A series of mirrors are positioned on the pathway between the chair's office and the adjoining administrator's office. This threshold is further marked by the removal of segments of the lay-in ceiling, retaining the spline grid and exposing mechanical systems. Perforated, angled planes are hung as a canopy and lit from above.

Throughout the piece materials are used for their referential qualities. The mirror, with its suggestion of private, domestic space, contrasts with the institutional setting. The fluted glass of the pocket door recalls institutional dividers; the velour upholstery, the neat decoration of a generation ago. Found materials such as chalk ledges and door sections are incorporated into the construction. Written texts pertaining to the history of the school are used as well. The words of Frank Parsons—about "race consciousness," the home, and the mission of the interior designer— are inscribed on the louvers of the pocket door. Three text plaques are also to be installed, one on the wall of the conference room, one each inlaid on the floors of the chair's office and staff room. These will bear inscriptions by John Dewey, the founders of the New School, and the following by Theodor Adorno: ". . . a stroke of undeserved luck has kept the mental composition of some individuals not quite adjusted to prevailing norms."

1991, project for permanent installation
Basswood, chipboard, silk
Department of Environmental Design, Parsons School of Design, New School for Social Research, New York, New York

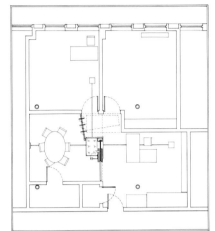

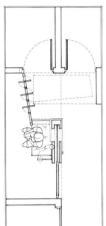

Framing American Cities

The following are preliminary studies for the exhibition Framing American Cities. This project abstracts familiar elements drawn from the urban landscape to represent three U.S. cities: New York; Columbus, Ohio; and San Francisco. It seeks to draw parallels between the form of cities and the evolution of American ideology.

Each of the three cities are represented by clusters of pieces or fields located within the gallery space.

The spacing and adjacency of each grouping relates to the disposition of cities along the plane of the United States. The viewer sees the nation in a promenade through the exhibition room. Each piece also functions as a viewing stand from which to see the other constructions. Mobile panels, affixed like rearview mirrors, provide framing devices. In addition aural fields are activated at each site, switched on and off with the random passage of viewers.

The floor of the exhibition space is gridded, with points of intersection marked by vertical wires, posts, and partial walls. This field becomes apparent as a network, at times extruded into three dimensions. The grid continues up the side wall. Objects project from this grid and from intermediate partitions.

The horizon is marked with a line at chair-rail height and completes the major crossing that divides the space. The ambiguity of the orientation of planes and of the reading of scale is encouraged.

Each of the cities shares formal elements with the other. The tower units of New York reappear in Columbus. The large frames of Columbus reappear in San Francisco. The fields of both cities at the edge overlap in the center, through the transparency of the grid.

1990, model
Basswood

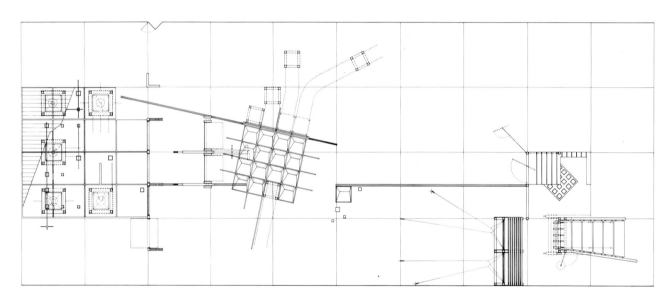

Installation plan

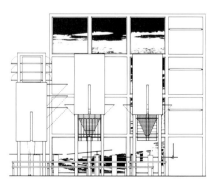

New York

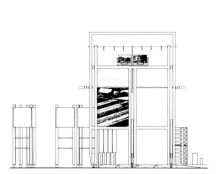

Columbus

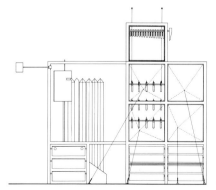

San Francisco

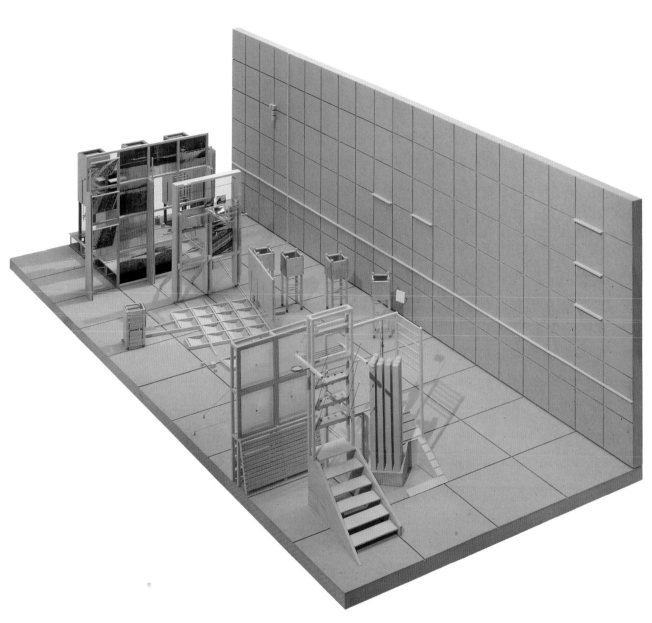

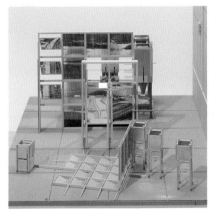

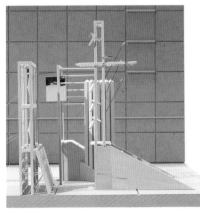

New York: Angle of Incidence

New York City is represented by five towers, six feet in height, like figures or armoires. Their placement on an elevated floor establishes a gridded field to be navigated by the viewer. The towers can be opened by sliding aside translucent rawhide sheaths, revealing louvered cavities above, and loudspeakers, television tubes, and wires below. The movement of the spectator and the manipulation of the towers control the access to video screens as they are raised up from below the metal computer subfloor.

Entering through a threshold of glass panes, the viewer trips a succession of four video images and six sound tracks. The first plays a repeating loop of the final stylized dance number from the 1932 movie *Forty-Second Street*, with sound alone, with sound and image, and with image alone. On the second screen is a series of black-and-white aerial views from a book on New York City. The scene changes every 15 seconds as a young Chilean woman, off-camera, reads passages from *How the Other Half Lives*, while turning pages of this book. The third screen is tuned to a local station: news programs, commercials, "Hawaii 5-0." A tape under the fourth tower plays a segment of Ives's Orchestral Set no. 2, 1917, abstracted from "In The Sweet By and By." Under the fifth, a radio is tuned to WBLS. Under the grating in the center of the platform, a video clip of Jeff Stryker in *Powertool* repeats without sound.

Opposite this analogue for the city are a series of habitable structures. Seats, stairs, and bleachers provide the viewer with positions for individual and collective observation. Cubicles and stalls are configured as low, modest enclosures like flexible office systems, confessionals, or peep show booths. These latter elements, behind canvas screens, provide settings that suggest the possibility of physical proximity, intimacy, and public interaction. A scale relation is implied between the inhabitation of these interior structures located behind the canvas screened room at the center of the gallery—like a larger tower—and the depiction of the underside of the city. Up a small flight of stairs the third scale of the tower is glimpsed in the actual city, north on Broadway toward the Chrysler Building, through a slot in the gallery wall.

The intention is to reveal the simultaneous city, the sites passed each day and seen only partially. Covered by nightfall or geography or reticence, the activities at the margin are hidden yet always open to inspection. These sites elude and are excluded from dominant representations of space and the culture that inhabits it. We see instead a children's tale, expurgated for all on television and billboards, a particular fiction of American life, set apart as in the floating world or carnival or the combat zone. The boundaries, which are selectively sanctioned and controlled, are co-opted in spaces left over. They are without current economic value, far enough away and out of sight.

1991, installation
Aluminum, canvas, wood, rawhide, TV monitors
The Clocktower Gallery, Institute for Contemporary Art, New York, New York

The Clocktower Gallery

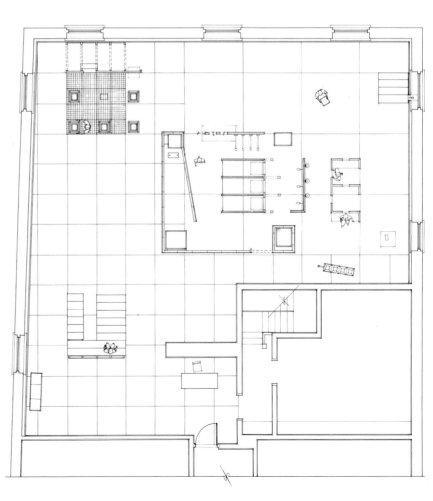

"This may seem obvious, but there is reason to believe that the traditional political landscape had a very different concept of a boundary: it was intended less to define a region and establish an effective relationship with the outside world than to isolate and protect something within it." [1]

TO OPERATE : GRASP
SHEATH FIRMLY AND
DEPRESS SLOWLY

"Every traditional public space, whether religious, political or ethnic in character, displays a variety of symbols, inscriptions, images, monuments, not as works of art but to remind people of their civic privileges and duties and tacitly exclude the outsider." [2]

"The streets are worn and stained like interiors. The steps, railings, hydrants, curbs have not aged with constant use over a long period of time. Rather they have been broken and damaged by violent successions, like a basin in a public lavatory, a cell door, a bed in a lodging house. Each sidewalk has a terrible intimacy. At street level in Manhattan there is no distinction whatsoever between intimate and public events." [3]

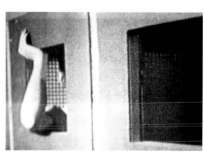

1. J. B. Jackson, *Discovering the Vernacular Landscape* (New Haven: Yale University Press, 1984), 14.
2. Ibid., 18.
3. John Berger, *Sense of Sight* (New York: Pantheon, 1985), 62.

Columbus: Expansion City

Placed in the center of the room, a representation of this city is seen through a series of viewing frames reminiscent of stereopticons. Collectively the objects imply a streetfront that forms a loosely defined center recessed into a raised floor. Each of the pieces, recalling nineteenth-century commercial blocks and corn cribs, is on wheels, allowing them to be moved by the viewer. One moves along orthogonal tracks, the rails of the west; others roll in the curved routes of exit ramps on the interstate. The elements along the constituted Main Street disperse leaving a void at the center. This mobility recalls Sartre's observation on the quality of the American city as un-rooted and light on the surface of the ground.

A representation of the plat of the town is set below a field of closely spaced sections of galvanized conduit with outlet boxes. They rise from the grid like corn, or RV hook-ups, or the potential connections for a subdivision. The current within is controlled by timed coin-operated devices, which allow the viewer to purchase short intervals of power and light. These electronic grids are expressions of communication, commerce, and the unlimited expansion of infrastructure on the horizontal plane—the non-industrial suburb of the evolving American city.

1992, installation
Asphalt shingles, wood, plastic, linoleum
Wexner Center for the Arts, Ohio State University, Columbus, Ohio

Public square

Wexner Center

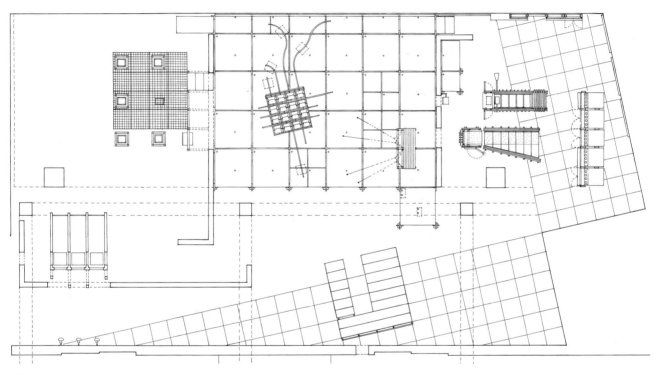

Installation plan

Grid of conduit and Ohio towers   View towards the east

San Francisco: Tented City of Men
Companion Piece

A tilted plane, like the drop of the Pacific Palisades, is split in two. Located at the end of the installation sequence, east to west, one of the wedges provides an elevated platform for the view back across the land. The viewer stands at the edge of this incline, positioned behind a screen of bobbing test-tubes filled with red, white, and yellow water. Looking forward, an aerial perspective is glimpsed through translucent fabric panels stretched through a vertical grid. The distance above allows for a coherence of the pattern to be read.

An upholstered plinth on which to recline is parallel to the viewing stand. It is equipped with a side chair for consultation or condolence set behind a pair of movable shutters. A mirror directs images from the other "cities" in through a small opening to the viewer on his or her back. Gazing up past this view is the ceiling—a series of hanging cloths or hankies suspended on hooks.

The long wall of the gallery receives wainscoting, shallow closets and shutters, which are repeated in a

freestanding louvered wall at the rear of the installation. This wall, supporting rows of blue specimen jars, obscures a panel of full-length mirrors, like a gym or dance studio. The shutters permit slatted views or swing open to windows and a door. Theatrical colored light, scrim, and a series of purple orchids are seen against reflections of viewers moving within a space suggestive of traditional domestic settings. There is a sense of the possibility to reinvent oneself at the edge, a continuously shifting line of frontier. In the case of San Francisco, a Victorian construction is reinhabited against the grain.

San Francisco was an instant city built quickly of canvas, the destination for single men in search of frontier and wealth. The city was rebuilt after successive natural disasters: fires, earthquakes, AIDS. This time, the buildings remain standing.

1992, installation
Wood, mirror, fabric
Wexner Center for the Arts,
Ohio State University,
Columbus, Ohio

SUNDRY AMUSEMENTS IN THE MINES.

A SUNDAYS AMUSEMENTS.

A DAILY PLEASURE.

OCCUPATION FOR RAINY DAYS.

A PLEASANT SURPRISE.

Mail sheets, ca. 1848

Bragg Plumbing, 1991

Viewing stand and recamier

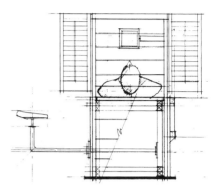

Recamier, section/elevation

After the 1906 earthquake

San Francisco wall

Photo Credits

Project Credits

Utopian Prospect
Assistance: Jess Walker, Ben Felix.
Dancers: John Austin Wiggins, Peter Richards.
Funded though the New York Foundation for the Arts and
The Woodstock Guild.

American Fictions
Assistance: Kevin Kemner, Bill Markland, Dan Grandy.
Dancer: Jeff Rigby.

Departmental Chair
Drawing: Steve Turk.
Model: Tom Easterson.

Winesburg
This work was undertaken with the support of the Chicago
Institute for Architecture and Urbanism during a residency at the
Charnley House.

Signs and Wonders
Assistants: Kevin Kemner, Mark Noltimier, Dan Grandy,
Chris Deihl.

Framing American Cities
Drawing: Mark Noltimier.
Model: Brian Sell.

New York: Angle of Incidence
Project Team: Tom Easterson, Stephen Turk, Tom Pitzen,
Mark Noltimier.
Assistance: Lewis Huffman, Lisa Tilder, Chris Deihl, Terri Kite,
Carla Trott, Jeff Hissem, Mohammed Karimnamazi, Eymen
Homsi, Sarah Bond.
Model: Brian Sell.
Drawing: Steve Turk.
Dancers: Jeff Rigby, Mac Springfield, Peggy Gould.
Funded in part by grants from The National Endowment for the
Arts, The New York State Council on the Arts, and The Ohio
State University.

Columbus, Ohio and San Francisco
Project Team: Diane Porthouse, Phil Rudy, Tom Pitzen, Lewis
Huffman, Maria Ramirez.
Assistance: Michael Williams, Tim Mizicko, Jeff Nelson, Steve
Turk, Jeff Hissem, Sean Murphy.
Funded In part through grants from The Ohio Arts Council,
The OSU Columbia Quincentenary Committee, The Ohio State
University, and the OSU Department of Architecture.

Exhibitions

Selected Solo Exhibitions

Framing American Cities, parts 1+2+3, Wexner Center for the Arts, Columbus, Ohio, 1992.

New York/Angles of Incidence: Framing American Cities, part 1, Clocktower Gallery, Institute for Contemporary Art, New York, NY, 1991.

Signs and Wonders, (with B. Gianni), Hewlett Gallery, Carnegie Mellon University, Pittsburgh, PA, 1991.

American Fictions, (with B. Gianni), John Nichols Gallery, New York, NY, 1989.

Utopian Prospect, Byrdcliffe Arts Colony, Woodstock, NY, 1988.

Selected Group Exhibitions

Paper as Knowledge, III International Bienalle, Leopold Hoesch Museum, Duren, West Germany, 1990.

Architects + Artifacts, Society for Art in Crafts, Pittsburgh, PA, 1990.

New Schools for New York, PEA/Architectural League, Urban Center Galleries, NY, 1990.

Bearings: Faculty Architecture in North America,

Parsons Exhibition Center, New York, NY; Princeton University, Princeton, NJ, 1988–89.

Firing the Imagination, Artists and Architects Collaboration, Urban Center Galleries, New York, NY, 1988.

Reweaving the Urban Fabric—International Approaches to Infill Housing, Paine-Webber Gallery, New York, NY, 1988.

Salvation Furniture, Grand Windows Project, Grand Central Station, New York, NY, 1988.

Vacant Lots, Infill Housing Study, NYHPD / Architectural League, Old Mercantile Exchange, New York, NY, 1987.

Room in the City, City Gallery, New York, NY; Catholic University, Washington, DC; Univ. of Kansas, Lawrence, KS, 1987–89.

For the Landscape, Public Image Gallery, New York, NY, 1987.

Natural History, Public Image Gallery, New York, NY, 1986.

Rough Drafts, Urban Center Gallery, New York, NY, 1985.

City Altars, "10 on 8" windows, New York, NY, 1983.

Terminal New York, Brooklyn Marine Terminal, New York, NY, 1983.

Reviews

Kipnis, Jeffrey. "Mark Robbins." A + U (September 1992): 44–60. (Three projects.)

McGrath, Brian. "Mark Robbins: Framing American Cities." *SITES* (January 1992): 118.

Dollens, Dennis. "Signs and Wonders." *SITES* (1992): 92–95.

Phillips, Patricia. "Mark Robbins." *Artforum* (January 1992): 107. (Framing American Cities.)

Allen, Stan. "Mark Robbins: Ambidextrous/Architecture." *Newsline* (November/December 1991): 7.

Barriere, Phillipe. "USA, D'est en Ouest." *L'Architecture d'Aujourd'Hui* (October 1990): 115.

Dollens, Dennis, ed. "American Fictions." *SITES* (1990): 92–95.

Fiske, E. B. "Lessons." *The New York Times* (21 February 1990): B8. (New Schools for New York.)

Shane, Graham. "Farm + City: Robbins + Gianni." *Architese* (February 1990): 78–79.

Prown, Lise. "Urban Ornamentalism." *Stroll* (June/July 1988): 80.

Shepard, Joan. "All in a Clay's Work." *New York Daily News* (18 February 1988).

Massello, David. "Design for Vacant Lots." *Metropolis* (March 1988): 24.

Strickland, Roy. "Infill Housing in New York." *Progressive Architecture* (January 1988): 37–38.

Goldberger, Paul. "Designs that Reach High for People with Low Incomes." *New York Times* (8 November 1987): 38.

Phillips, Patricia. "Room in the City." *Artforum* (September 1987): 131.

Goldberger, Paul. "Bringing Light and Space to a Tenement." *New York Times* (3 May 1987).

Sorkin, Michael. "Room in the City." *The Village Voice* (19 May 1987): 83.

Bolles, Daralice. "Finding Room in the City." *Progressive Architecture* (June 1987): 25.

Geibel, Victoria. "Compressed Living." *Metropolis* (April 1987): 47, 51.

Geibel, Victoria. "Builders of the Future." *Metropolis* (October 1986).

Geibel, Victoria. "Remembrance of Things Past." *Metropolis* (June 1986): 15.

Massello, David. "Building Their Reputations." *Interview* (October 1985): 87–88.

Publications

Genevro, Rosalie ed. *New Schools for New York.* New York: Princeton Architectural Press/The Architectural League, 1992.

Robbins, Mark. "Framing American Cities." *Design Quarterly* 151(1991).

Linsey and Rosenblatt, eds. *Architects and Artifacts.* Pittsburgh, PA: Society for Art in Crafts,1991.

Bearings. New York: Princeton Architectural Press/Parsons School of Design, 1991.

Willis, Carol and Rosalie Genevro, eds. *Vacant Lots.* New York: Princeton Architectural Press/The Architectural League, 1991.

Robbins, Mark. "Growing Pains, An American Suburb in Middle Age," *Metropolis* (October 1988): 72–79, 112, 114, 117, 119.

Robbins, Mark. "Gardens Under Glass, Public Amenity Spaces in NYC," *Metropolis* (May 1987): 56–58, 63, 65, 67, 101.

Beeler, Ray, ed. *Room in the City.* New York: Princeton Architectural Press, 1987.